Let's Keep in Touch

Follow US   Online

Visit US at

www.learnpersianonline.com

Call

1-469-230-3605

 www.facebook.com/PersiaClubCo

 www.twitter.com/PersiaClub

 www.instagram.com/LearnPersianOnline

Online Persian Lessons via Skype

It's easy! Here's how it works.

1- Request a FREE introductory session.

2- Meet a Persian tutor online via Skype.

3- Start speaking Real Persian in Minutes.

Send Email to: info@LearnPersianOnline.com

Or Call: **+1-469-230-3605**

www.learnpersianonline.com

... So Much More Online!

FREE Persian lessons

More Persian learning books!

Online Persian – English Dictionary

Online Persian Tutors

Looking for an Online Persian Tutor?

Call us at: 001-469-230-3605

Send email to: Info@ learnpersianonline.com

Read and Write Persian Language in 7 Days

A Workbook

and

Step-by-Step Guide

By

Reza Nazari & Somayeh Nazari

Copyright © 2016

Reza Nazari & Somayeh Nazari

All rights reserved.No part of this publication may be reproduced, stored in a retrieval system, or transmitted in any form or by any means, electronic, mechanical, photocopying, recording, scanning, or otherwise, except as permitted under Section 107 or 108 of the 1976 United States Copyright Ac, without permission of the author.

All inquiries should be addressed to:

info@learnpersianonline.com

www.learnpersianonline.com

ISBN-13: 978-1537387949

ISBN-10: 1537387944

Published by: Learn Persian Online Website

www.learnpersianonline.com

About Learn Persian Online Website

The *"Learn Persian Online Website"* was founded on the belief that everyone interested in Persian language should have the opportunity to learn it!

Established in 2012 and conveniently located in Dallas, Texas, the *"Learn Persian Online Website"* creates international opportunities for all people interested in Persian language and culture and builds trust between them. We believe in this cultural relation!

If you are intended to learn more about Persian, this beautiful language and culture, *"Learn Persian Online Website"* is your best starting point. Our highly qualified Persian experts can help you connect to Persian culture and gain confidence you need to communicate effectively in Persian.

Over the past few years, our professional instructors, unique online resources and publications have helped thousands of Persian learners and students improve their language skills. As a result, these students have gained their goals faster. We love celebrating those victories with our students.

Please view our website at:

www.learnpersianonline.com

About the Author

Reza Nazari is a Persian author. He has published more than 100 Persian learning books including "Persia Club Dictionary Persian – English" and "Learn Farsi in 100 Days".

Reza is also a professional Persian teacher. Over the past eight years, his online Persian classes have helped thousands of Persian learners and students around the world improve their language skills effectively.

To participate in online Persian classes or ask questions about learning Persian, you can contact Reza via email at:

reza@learnpersianonline.com

Description

This book helps you learn how to write and read in Persian Language in a fast and fun way. You can quickly begin to read, pronounce and write in Persian. The book proceeds step-by-step through all the letters of the Persian alphabet, displaying the sounds they stand for and how they are written in words. In addition to the alphabet, you'll learn basic grammar, sentence structures, and pronunciation. Beyond grammar and alphabet lessons, you will also find comprehensive listings of most common Persian words as well as useful tables that you can use as quick references to speed up your mastery of the language.

This book aims to provide a solid foundation on learning the Persian language by providing simple grammar rules while enriching vocabulary and comprehension with useful and practical phrases. It is designed to address the needs of Persian students, travelers, and self-learners who need to have a working knowledge of Persian in a few days' time.

The book *"Read and Write Persian Language in 7 Days"* is incredibly useful for those who want to learn Persian language quickly and efficiently.

You'll be surprised how fast you master the first steps in learning this beautiful language!

Contents

Pronunciation 11

Persian Alphabet 13

1st Day: Most Common Persian Letters 17

    Persian Vowels 35

2nd Day: Let's Make Sentences 39

3rd Day: Let's Learn Persian Grammar 63

4th Day: Persian Adjectives 89

5th Day: More Common Persian Words 114

6th Day: Let's Count in Persian 138

7st Day: Time to Read in Persian 149

Exercise Answers 165

Glossary 174

Appendix 1

  Most Common Persian Verbs 2

  Persian Most Common Words 11

    Family 11

    Weather 14

    Colors 201

    Animals 203

    Fruits/Vegetables 21

    Jobs 24

IX   www.LearnPersianOnline.com

X www.LearnPersianOnline.com

Pronunciation

The regular letters used for written Persian stand for some different sounds. It is usually difficult to tell how a word is pronounced just by looking at how it is spelled. Therefore, it is useful to show the pronunciation of each word separately, using a system of symbols in which each symbol stands for one sound only. The pronunciations of letters and words are given within two slashes.

This book uses a simple spelling system to show how letters and words are pronounced, using the symbols listed below.

Symbol	Example	Symbol	Example
a	hat /hat	m	move /muv
â	cut / cât	n	need /nid
ay	time /tâym	o	gorgeous /gorjes
ch	church	ô	coat/ côt
d	dog /dâg	u	mood /mud
e	men /men	p	park /park
ey	name /neym	r	rise /rais
f	free /fri	s	seven /seven
g	get /get	n	nation /neishen
h	his /hiz	t	train /treyn
i	feet /fit	v	vary /vari
iyu	cute /kiyut	y	yet /yet
j	jeans /jinz	z	zipper /zipper
k	key /ki	zh	measure /mezher/
kh	loch /lakh	ʻ	تعظیم / ta'zim
l	loss /lâs	gh	sound "r" in French word "Paris"

Persian Alphabet

The Persian alphabet (Persian: الفبای فارسی) consists 32 letters, most of which have two forms, short and full. In Persian, words are written from right to left while numbers are written from left to right. Persian is a writing style based on the Arabic script. It is entirely written cursively. That is, the majority of letters in a word connect to each other. Therefore, the appearance of a letter changes depending on its position: beginning (joined on the left), middle (joined on both sides), end (joined on the right) of a word and some letters are written isolated.

This writing style is also implemented on computers. Whenever the Persian script is typed, the computer connects the letters to each other.

Following is a table showing the Persian alphabet and how it is pronounced in English. There are also some examples of how those letters would sound if you place them in a word.

	Persian Alphabet			اَلفبای فارسی	
Row	Letters	Pronunciation	Sample	Pronunciation	Meaning
1.	ا - آ	alef	آب	āb	water
2.	بـ - ب	be	بابا	bābā	father
3.	پـ - پ	pe	پاپ	pāp	the pope
4.	تـ - ت	te	تاب	tāb	swing
5.	ثـ - ث	se	اَثاث	asās	furniture
6.	جـ - ج	jim	تاج	tāj	crown
7.	چـ - چ	che	چای	chāi	tea
8.	حـ - ح	he	حَج	haj	pilgrimage
9.	خـ - خ	khe	خانه	khāneh	home
10.	د	dāl	دَرد	dard	pain
11.	ذ	zāl	جَذب	jazb	absorption
12.	ر	re	دَر	dar	door
13.	ز	ze	میز	miz	table
14.	ژ	zhe	ژاپُن	zhāpon	japan
15.	سـ - س	sin	اُستاد	ostād	professor

	Persian Alphabet			آلفبای فارسی	
Row	Letters	Pronunciation	Sample	Pronunciation	Meaning
16.	شـ - ش	shin	دانشجو	dāneshjoo	student
17.	صـ - ص	sād	صَد	sad	hundred
18.	ضـ - ض	zād	وُضو	vozu	ablution
19.	ط	tā	طَناب	tanāb	rope
20.	ظ	zā	ظُهر	zohr	noon
21.	عـ - ع	eyn	عَدَد	adad	number
22.	غـ - غ	gheyn	شُغل	shoghl	job
23.	فـ - ف	fe	دَفتَر	daftar	notebook
24.	قـ - ق	ghāf	قَهوه	ghahveh	coffee
25.	کـ - ک	kāf	کِتاب	ketāb	book
26.	گـ - گ	gāf	دانشگاه	dāneshgāh	university
27.	لـ - ل	lâm	کِلاس	kelās	classroom
28.	مـ - م	mim	مات	māt	blur
29.	نـ - ن	nun	نان	nān	bread
30.	و	vāv	وان	vān	bath

	Persian Alphabet			آلفبای فارسی	
Row	Letters	Pronunciation	Sample	Pronunciation	Meaning
31.	هـ ـهـ ـه	he	ماه	māh	moon
32.	یـ - ی	ye	نیم	nim	half

ا – آ

Name: "آ - ا", called "alef", is the first letter of the Persian alphabet.

Form: Letter "alef" has two forms:

"آ" It is an initial letter which never joins the following and preceding letters. Final "alef" is written as "ا". It joins only the preceding letters.

Sound: "آ" always pronouns /â/ like "a" in "father".

"ا" has four sounds, /â/ like "a" in "father", /a/ like "a" in "cat", /e/ like "e" in "men", and /o/ like "o" in "gorgeous".

How to write it:

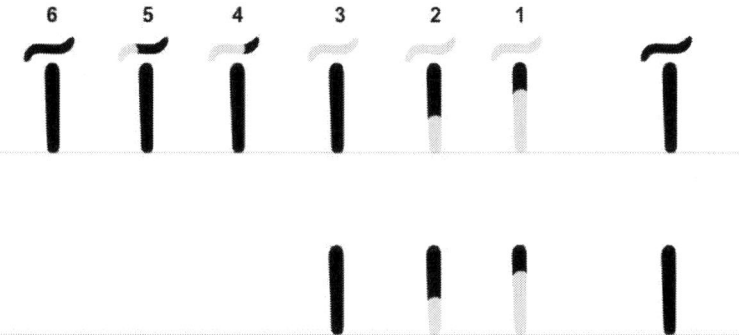

Exercise: Let's practice! Write on the letters.

آ : آ ـ آ ـ آ ـ آ ـ آ ـ آ ـ آ ـ آ ـ آ ـ آ ـ آ

آ ـ آ ـ آ ـ آ ـ آ ـ آ ـ آ ـ آ ـ آ ـ آ ـ آ ـ آ

ا : ا ـ ا ـ ا ـ ا ـ ا ـ ا ـ ا ـ ا ـ ا ـ ا ـ ا ـ ا

ا ـ ا ـ ا ـ ا ـ ا ـ ا ـ ا ـ ا ـ ا ـ ا ـ ا ـ ا ـ ا

Name: "ب - بـ" /be/ is the second letter of the Persian alphabet.

Sound: It sounds /be/ like "b" in "black".

Form: "بـ - ب" has two forms. "بـ" is the short form and "ب" is the full form.

Notice: In general, letters in short forms take the initial or medial positions in a Persian word. Letters in full form come only at the end of the words.

How to write it:

Sample Words:

آب /âb/: water

بابا /bâbâ/: dad

با /bâ/: with - by

Exercise: Practice the letters.

ب : بْ - بْ - بْ - بْ - بْ - بْ - بْ - بْ

ب : بْ - بْ - بْ - بْ - بْ - بْ - بْ - بْ

Improve Your Writing: Write on the sample words

آب: آبْ - آبْ - آبْ - آبْ - آبْ - آبْ

بابا: بابا - بابا - بابا - بابا - بابا - بابا

آب: آبْ - آبْ - آبْ - آبْ - آبْ - آبْ

بابا: بابا - بابا - بابا - بابا - بابا - بابا

Name: "ن – نـ" called "nun", is the twenty-ninth letter of the Persian alphabet.

Form: It has short and full forms.

Sound: "ن" sounds /ne/ like "n" in "noon".

How to write it:

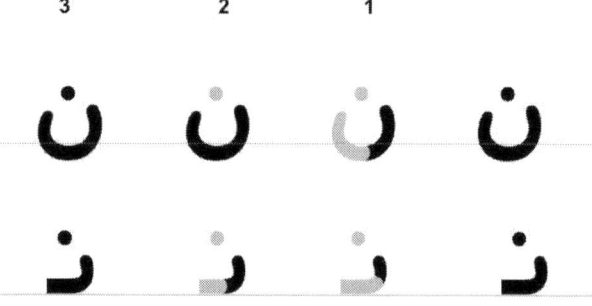

Sample Words:

نان /nân/: bread

بَنا /banâ/: building

آن /ân/: that - it

Exercise: Practice the letter.

نـ: نـ – نـ – نـ – نـ – نـ – نـ – نـ – نـ – نـ

ن: ن – ن – ن – ن – ن – ن – ن – ن – ن

Improve Your Writing: Write on the sample words.

نان: نان – نان – نان – نان – نان – نان – نان – نان

بنا: بنا – بنا – بنا – بنا – بنا – بنا – بنا – بنا

د

Name: "د" /dâl/ is the tenth letter of the Persian alphabet.

Sound: It sounds /de/ like "d" in "dog".

Form: It only has one form. "د" only joins the preceding letters in Persian words.

How to write it

2   1

د   د   د

Sample Words:

باد /bâd/: wind   بَد /bad/ : bad

بَدَن /badan/: body   داد /dâd/: shout

                          دادَن /dâdan/: to give

Exercise: Practice the letters.

د: د – د – د – د – د – د – د – د – د – د

د – د – د – د – د – د – د – د – د – د

Improve Your Writing: Write on the sample words

داد: داد – داد – داد – داد – داد – داد

داد – داد – داد – داد – داد – داد

ر

Name: "ر" /re/ is the twelfth letter of the Persian alphabet.

Sound: It sounds /re/ like "r" in "red".

Form: It has one format. "ر" only joins to the preceding letters in Persian words.

How to write it

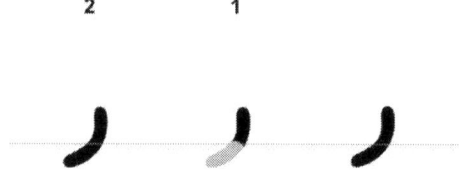

Sample Words

pomegranate /anâr/: اَنار

door, in /dar/: دَر

rain /bârân/: باران

load /bâr/: بار

flour /ârd/: آرد

to drive /rândan/: راندَن

she/he has /dârad/: دارَد

/nadârad/: نَدارَد

she/he doesn't have

Sample Sentences:

بابا اَنار دارَد.[1]

بابا اَنار نَدارَد.

---

[1] translation: father has pomegranate.

Exercise: Practice the letters.

ر: ر – ر – ر – ر – ر – ر – ر – ر – ر – ر

ر – ر – ر – ر – ر – ر – ر – ر – ر

Improve Your Writing: Write on the sample words.

آرد: آرد – آرد – آرد – آرد – آرد – آرد

آرد – آرد – آرد – آرد – آرد – آرد – آرد

باران: باران – باران – باران – باران

باران – باران – باران – باران – باران

بار: بار – بار – بار – بار – بار – بار

بار – بار – بار – بار – بار – بار

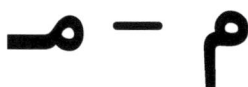

Name: "م – ـم" called "mim", is the twenty eighth letter of the Persian alphabet.

Sound: "م" sounds /me/ like "m" in "must".

Forms: It has short and full forms. "م" is the full form and "ـم" is the short form.

How to write it

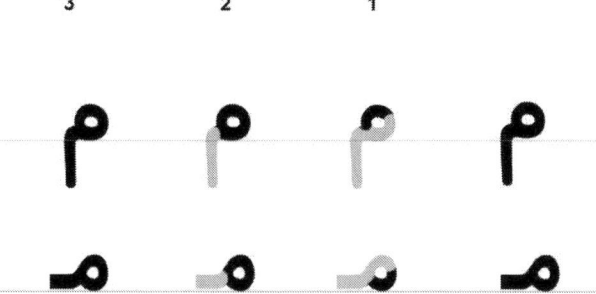

Sample Words:

نام /nâm/: name   بادام /bâdâm/: almond

دارَم /dâram/: I have   مادَر /mâdar/: mother

آمَدَم /âmadam/: I came   مار /mâr/: snake

آمَد /âmad/: he/she came   مَن /man/: I

مَرد /mard/: man

Sample Sentences:

مَن بادام دارَم.

آن مَرد بادام نَدارَد.

مَن دَر باران آمَدَم.

Exercise: Practice the letters.

مـ: مـ ‒ مـ ‒ مـ ‒ مـ ‒ مـ ‒ مـ ‒ مـ ‒ مـ ‒ مـ ‒ مـ

مـ ‒ مـ ‒ مـ ‒ مـ ‒ مـ ‒ مـ ‒ مـ ‒ مـ ‒ مـ ‒ مـ

م: م ‒ م ‒ م ‒ م ‒ م ‒ م ‒ م ‒ م ‒ م ‒ م ‒ م

م ‒ م ‒ م ‒ م ‒ م ‒ م ‒ م ‒ م ‒ م ‒ م ‒ م

Improve Your Writing: Write on the sample words.

مار: مار ‒ مار ‒ مار ‒ مار ‒ مار ‒ مار ‒ مار

مار ‒ مار ‒ مار ‒ مار ‒ مار ‒ مار ‒ مار

مادر: مادر ‒ مادر ‒ مادر ‒ مادر ‒ مادر

مادر ‒ مادر ‒ مادر ‒ مادر ‒ مادر ‒ مادر

بادام: بادام ‒ بادام ‒ بادام ‒ بادام ‒ بادام

بادام ‒ بادام ‒ بادام ‒ بادام ‒ بادام

س – سـ

Name: "س – سـ" called "sin", is the fifteenth letter of the Persian alphabet.

Sound: "س" sounds /se/ like "s" in "seven".

Form: It has two forms, short and full.

How to write it

3   2   1

س س س س

سـ سـ سـ سـ

Sample Words

سَر /sar/: head   داس /dâs/: sickle

سَردَرد /sardard/: headache   سَبَد /sabad/: basket

سَم /sam/: poison   اَسب /asb/: horse

Sample Sentences:

بابا اَسب دارَد.

آن مَرد با اَسب آمَد.

مادَر سَبد دارَد.

مَن سَردَرد دارَم.

Exercise: Practice the letters.

سـ: سـ – سـ – سـ – سـ – سـ – سـ – سـ – سـ

سـ – سـ – سـ – سـ – سـ – سـ – سـ – سـ – سـ

س: س – س – س – س – س – س – س – س

س – س – س – س – س – س – س – س – س – س

Improve Your Writing: Write on the sample words.

اسب: اسب – اسب – اسب – اسب – اسب

اسب – اسب – اسب – اسب – اسب

سبد: سبد – سبد – سبد – سبد – سبد

سبد – سبد – سبد – سبد – سبد

داس: داس – داس – داس – داس – داس

داس – داس – داس – داس – داس

Persian Vowels

Persian language has six simple vowels, three short vowels and three long vowels:

Short vowels:

1- short vowel ─── a   as in English "that"

2- Short vowel ─── e   as in English "men"

3- Short vowel ─── o   as in English "code"

Example:

/ba/ بَ   /na/ نَ   /ma/ مَ

/be/ بِ   /ne/ نِ   /me/ مِ

/bo/ بُ   /no/ نُ   /mo/ مُ

Short vowels are written with other letters, above or below them:

مَرد /mard/: man

سَبَد /sabad/: basket

Three short vowel signs are not usually used in writing. They sometimes are written at elementary stages of learning to help learners understand the sound of Persian words.

Long vowels:

4- Long vowel آ â as in English "car"

5- Long vowel ای i as in English "fit"

6- Long vowel او u as in English "foot"

Three letters of آ /â/ - ای /i/ - او /u/ are used for writing three long vowels:

با / bâ/   بَ / ba/

بی /bi/   بِ /be/

بو /bu/   بُ /bo/

نا /nâ/   نَ /na/

نی /bi/   نِ /ne/

نو /nu/   نُ /no/

Exercise 1: Join the letters and read the words:

١. ب + د + ن

....

٢. ب + ا + ر + ا + ن

....

٣. ب + ا + د + ا + م

....

٤. س + ب + د

....

Exercise 2: Read the words and write in Persian.

1. nân ....

2. bad....................

3. anâr....................

4. mard..................

5. sar ....

6. mâdar ....

7. nâm ....

8. asb ....

9. bârân ....

10. ârd ....

2nd Day:

Let's Make Sentences

ت - تـ

Name: "تـ = ت" /te/ is the fourth letter of the Persian alphabet.

Sound: It sounds /te/ like "T" in "Train".

Form: It has two forms. "تـ" is the short form and "ت" is the full form.

How to write it

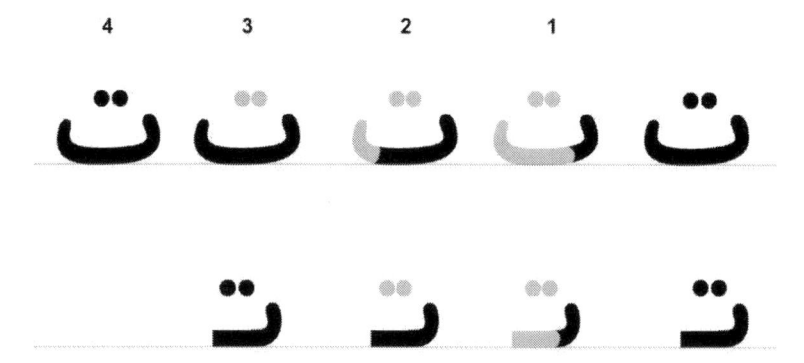

Sample Words

راست /râst/: right   تاب /tâb/: swing

مَتن /matn/: text   تَب /tab/: fever

تَبَر /tabar/: chopper   دَست /dast/: hand

اَست /ast/: is

Sample Sentences:

آن سَبَد اَست.

مَن تَب دارَم.

سارا تاب دارَد.

آن اَنار اَست.

Exercise: Practice the letters.

ت: ـت – ـت – ـت – ـت – ـت – ـت – ـت – ـت – ـت

ـت – ـت – ـت – ـت – ـت – ـت – ـت – ـت – ـت

ت: ت – ت – ت – ت – ت – ت – ت – ت – ت

ت – ت – ت – ت – ت – ت – ت – ت – ت

Improve Your Writing: Write on the sample words.

تا: تا – تا – تا – تا – تا – تا – تا – تا – تا

تا – تا – تا – تا – تا – تا – تا – تا – تا

تب: تب – تب – تب – تب – تب – تب – تب – تب

تب – تب – تب – تب – تب – تب – تب – تب

تاب: تاب – تاب – تاب – تاب – تاب – تاب – تاب

تاب – تاب – تاب – تاب – تاب – تاب – تاب

ک - ک

Name: "ک - ک" called "kâf", is the twenty fifth letter of the Persian alphabet.

Sound: "ک" sounds /ke/ like "k" in "kettle".

Form: It has short and full forms.

How to write it

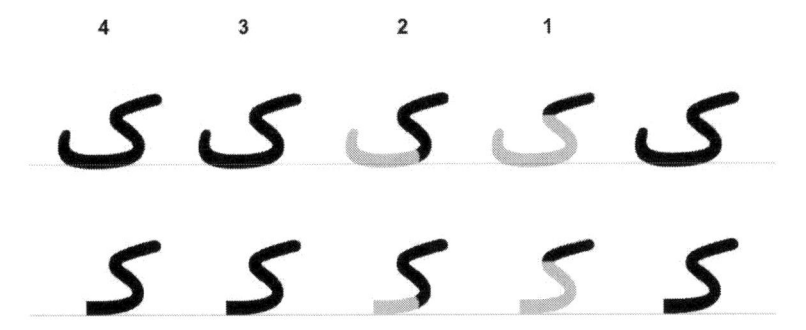

      4   3   2   1

ک ک ک ک ک

ک ک ک ک ک

Sample Words

کِتاب /ketāb/: book   کار /kâr/: deaf

کار /kār/: work   کَباب /kabāb/: kebab

کَم /kam/: little   کارمَند /kārmand/: employee

Sample Sentences:

آن کَباب اَست.

آن مَرد کَر اَست.

مَن کِتاب دارَم.

Exercise: Practice the letters.

ک: ک - ک - ک - ک - ک - ک - ک - ک

ک: ک - ک - ک - ک - ک - ک - ک - ک

Improve Your Writing: Write on the sample words.

کباب: کباب - کباب - کباب - کباب - کباب

کباب - کباب - کباب - کباب - کباب

کر: کر - کر - کر - کر - کر - کر - کر - کر

کر - کر - کر - کر - کر - کر - کر

کم: کم - کم - کم - کم - کم - کم - کم

کم - کم - کم - کم - کم - کم - کم

ز

Name: "ز" /ze/ is the thirteenth letter of the Persian alphabet.

Sound: It sounds /ze/ like "ze" in "zipper".

Form: It only has one form. "ز" only joins to the preceding letters in Persian words.

How to write it

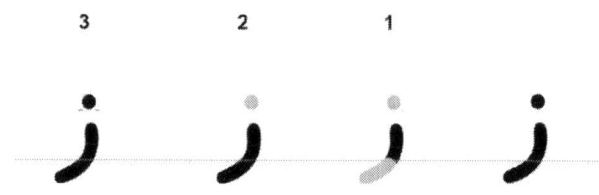

3   2   1

ز   ز   ز

Sample Words

بازار /bâzâr/: market   اَرز /arz/: currency

باز /bâz/: open   زَر /zar/: gold

زَبان /zabân/: language   بُز /boz/: goat

اَز /az/: from - of

Sample Sentences:

این بُز اَست.[1]

مادَر اَز بازار آمَد.[2]

---

[1] This is a goat.

[2] Mother came from bazaar.

Exercise: Practice the letters.

ژ: ژ – ژ – ژ – ژ – ژ – ژ – ژ – ژ – ژ – ژ

ژ – ژ – ژ – ژ – ژ – ژ – ژ – ژ – ژ – ژ

Improve Your Writing: Write on the sample words.

بژ: بژ – بژ – بژ – بژ – بژ – بژ – بژ – بژ – بژ

بژ – بژ – بژ – بژ – بژ – بژ – بژ – بژ – بژ

ارژ: ارژ – ارژ – ارژ – ارژ – ارژ – ارژ – ارژ – ارژ

ارژ – ارژ – ارژ – ارژ – ارژ – ارژ – ارژ – ارژ

ژر: ژر – ژر – ژر – ژر – ژر – ژر – ژر – ژر – ژر

ژر – ژر – ژر – ژر – ژر – ژر – ژر – ژر – ژر

ی - یـ

Name: "یـ - ی" /ye/ is the thirty second letter of the Persian alphabet.

Sound: It has three sounds, /ye/ like "y" in "yes", /e/ like "e" in "men", and /i/ like "ee" in "meet".

Form: "ی" has three forms. "یـ" is the short form and "ی" is the full format. "ی" sometimes is written as "ای" and sounds /i/ like "i" in "trip".

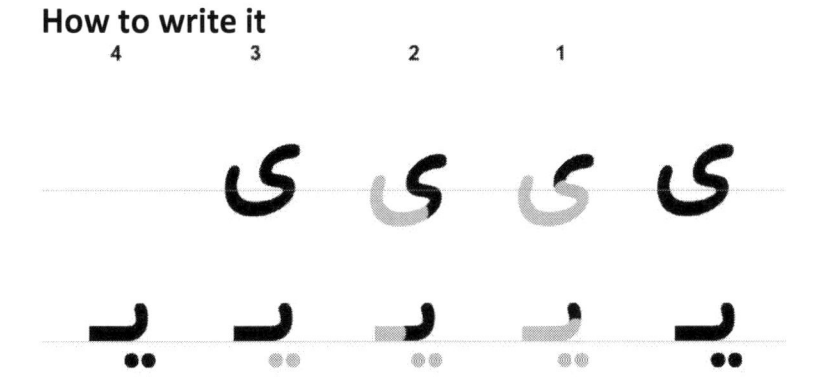

How to write it

4   3   2   1

Sample Words

بیمار /bimâr/: patient   سینی /sini/: tray

بیست /bist/: twenty   سیب /sib/: apple

یِک /yek/: one   بیدار /bidâr/: awake

سَبزی /sabzi/: vegetable

Sample Sentences

این سینی اَست.

مَن سیب دارَم.

مادَر بیمار اَست.

Exercise: Practice the letters.

یـ: یـ - یـ - یـ - یـ - یـ - یـ - یـ - یـ - یـ

یـ - یـ - یـ - یـ - یـ - یـ - یـ - یـ - یـ

ی: ی - ی - ی - ی - ی - ی - ی - ی - ی

ی - ی - ی - ی - ی - ی - ی - ی - ی

Improve Your Writing: Write on the sample words.

بیدار: بیدار - بیدار - بیدار - بیدار - بیدار

بیدار - بیدار - بیدار - بیدار - بیدار

سیب: سیب - سیب - سیب - سیب - سیب

سیب - سیب - سیب - سیب - سیب

سینی: سینی - سینی - سینی - سینی - سینی

سینی - سینی - سینی - سینی - سینی

Grammar Lesson

Simple Present of "to have"

دار + (م، ی، د، یم، ید، ند)

دارَم /dâram/: I have

داری /dâri/: You (singular) have

دارَد /dârad/: She/ he has

داریم /dârim/: We have

دارید /dârid/: You (plural) have

دارَند /dârand/: They have

Negative format of "to have"

Negative prefix "نَ" change the positive verbs to negative.

نَ + دار + (م، ی، د، یم، ید، ند)

نَدارَم /nadâram/: I don't have

نَداری /nadâri/: You (singular) don't have

نَدارَد /nadârad/: She/he doesn't have

نَداریم /nadârim/: We don't have

نَدارید /nadârid/: You (plural) don't have

نَدارَند /nadârand/: They don't have

و

Name: "و" called "vâv", is the thirtieth letter of the Persian alphabet.

Sound: It only has one form.

Form: "و" has three sounds. It sounds /v/ like "v" in "Very", sounds /o/ like "O" in "Orange", sounds /u/ like "oo" in "Good". "و" only joins to the preceding letters in Persian words.

How to write it

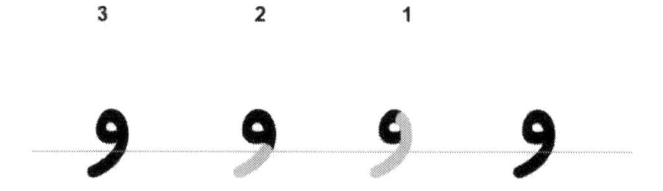

3 2 1

و و و و

Sample Words

دور /dur/: far

رود /rud/: river

تو /to/: you

او /u/: he – she

دوست /dust/: friend, like

دوست داری /dust dâri/:
You like it.

توت /tut/: berry

کور /kur/: blind

Sample Sentences:

سارا با زَری دوست اَست.

مادَر سارا را دوست دارَد.

تو توت دوست داری.

Exercise: Practice the letters.

و: و – و – و – و – و – و – و – و – و – و

و – و – و – و – و – و – و – و – و – و

Improve Your Writing: Write on the sample words.

توت: توت – توت – توت – توت – توت

توت – توت – توت – توت – توت

دوست: دوست – دوست – دوست – دوست

دوست – دوست – دوست – دوست

توپ: توپ – توپ – توپ – توپ – توپ

توپ – توپ – توپ – توپ – توپ

پ - پ

Name: "پ - پ" /pe/ is the third letter of the Persian alphabet.

Sound: It sounds /pe/ like "p" in "pen".

Form: "پ" has two forms. "پ" is the short form; therefore, it takes the initial or medial positions in a Persian word. "پ" is the full form. Therefore, it comes only at the end of the words.

How to write it

Sample Words

پَرواز /parvâz/: flight   پاپ /pâp/: the Pope

پَریدَن /paridan/: to jump   پا /pâp/: leg

پُر /por/: full   پوست /pust/: skin

Sample Sentences:

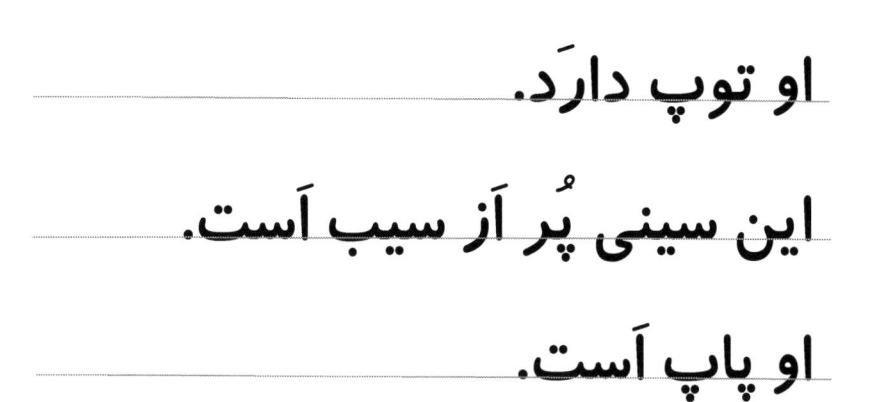

او توپ دارَد.

این سینی پُر اَز سیب اَست.

او پاپ اَست.

Exercise: Practice the letters.

پ : پـ ـ پـ ـ پـ ـ پـ ـ پـ ـ پـ ـ پـ ـ پـ

پـ ـ پـ ـ پـ ـ پـ ـ پـ ـ پـ ـ پـ ـ پـ ـ پـ

پ: ـپ ـ ـپ ـ ـپ ـ ـپ ـ ـپ ـ ـپ ـ ـپ ـ ـپ

ـپ ـ ـپ ـ ـپ ـ ـپ ـ ـپ ـ ـپ ـ ـپ ـ ـپ ـ ـپ

Improve Your Writing: Write on the sample words.

پا: پا ـ پا ـ پا ـ پا ـ پا ـ پا ـ پا ـ پا

پا ـ پا ـ پا ـ پا ـ پا ـ پا ـ پا ـ پا ـ پا

پاپ: پاپ ـ پاپ ـ پاپ ـ پاپ ـ پاپ ـ

پاپ ـ پاپ ـ پاپ ـ پاپ ـ پاپ ـ پاپ

Reading

آن سَبَد اَست.

آن سَبَد پُر اَز اَنار اَست.

این سینی اَست.

این سینی پُر اَز توت اَست.

Exercise 1: Join the letters and read the words:

۱. د + س + ت ....

۲. ک + ا + ر + م + ن + د ....

۳. ب + ا + ز + ا + ر ....

۴. د + و + س + ت ....

Exercise 2: Read the words and write in Persian.

1- matn .... 6- bidâr ....

2- ketāb .... 7- tut ....

3- kam .... 8- rud ....

4- zabân .... 9- parvâz ....

5- bimâr .... 10- por ....

3rd Day:

Let's Learn

Persian Grammar

ه ‒ ـه

Name: "ه ‒ ـهـ ‒ ـه" called "he", is the thirty first letter of the Persian alphabet.

Sound: It sounds /he/ like "h" in "hat". It also sounds /e/ like "e" in "men".

Form: "ه" is written in four forms:

Initial letter: ها   /hâ/   plural suffix

Medial letter: پَهن   /pahn/   wide

Final joined letter: تَپِه   /tapeh/   hill

Final disjoined letter: دَه   /dah/   ten

How to write it

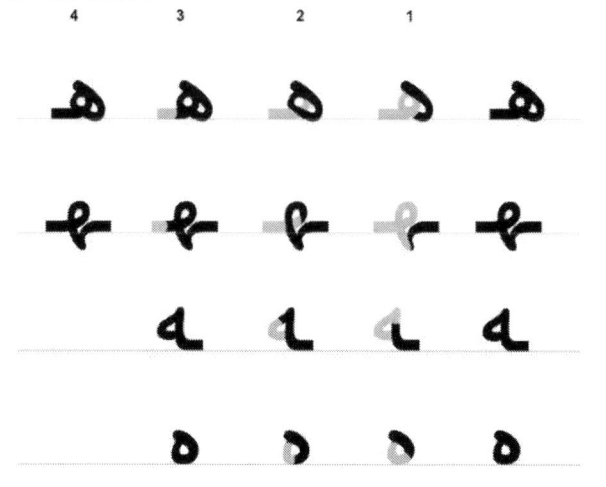

              4   3   2   1

Sample Words

star :/setâre/ ستاره   moon – month :/mâh/ ماه

artist :/honarmand/ هُنَرمَند   kind :/mehrabân/ مِهرَبان

letter: /nâme/ نامه   three :/se/ سه

       school :/madrese/ مَدرِسه

Sample Sentences

آن ستاره اَست.

مادَرِ مهرَبان اَست.

او هُنَرمَند اَست.

این نامهِ اَست.

Exercise: Practice the letters.

هـ : ـه - ـه - ـه - ـه - ـه - ـه - ـه - ـه - ـه

ـهـ : ـهـ - ـهـ - ـهـ - ـهـ - ـهـ - ـهـ - ـهـ - ـهـ

ه : ه - ه - ه - ه - ه - ه - ه - ه - ه

Improve Your Writing: Write on the sample words.

هدف: هدف – هدف – هدف – هدف - هدف

هدف: هدف – هدف – هدف – هدف - هدف

مهربان: مهربان – مهربان – مهربان - مهربان

مهربان: مهربان – مهربان – مهربان - مهربان

ماه: ماه – ماه – ماه – ماه – ماه – ماه

ماه: ماه – ماه – ماه – ماه – ماه – ماه

Grammar Lesson

Personal pronouns

There are six personal pronouns in Persian:

مَن /man/: I

تو /to/: You (singular)

او /u/: He / She

ما /mâ/: We

شُما /shomâ/: You (plural)

آنها /ânhâ/: They

Plural of nouns

"ان" and "ها" are the plural suffix in Persian.

nouns	Plural of nouns	
مادَر /mâdar/: mother	مادَران /mâdarân/	مادَرها /mâdarhâ/
اُستاد /ostâd/: teacher	اُستادان /ostâdân/	اُستادها /ostâdhâ/
ایرانی /irâni/: Iranian	ایرانیان /irâniyân/	ایرانی ها /irânihâ/

"ها" can be used for almost all Persian nouns but "ان" cannot be used for some Persian nouns.

Plural of nouns

کِتاب /Ketāb/   کِتابها /Ketāb/   کِتابان (incorrect)
book

$$خ - خ$$

Name: "خ – خ" /khe/ is the ninth letter of the Persian alphabet.

Sound: "خ" sounds /khe/ like "ch" in "loch", a Scottish word.

Form: It has short and full forms.

How to write it

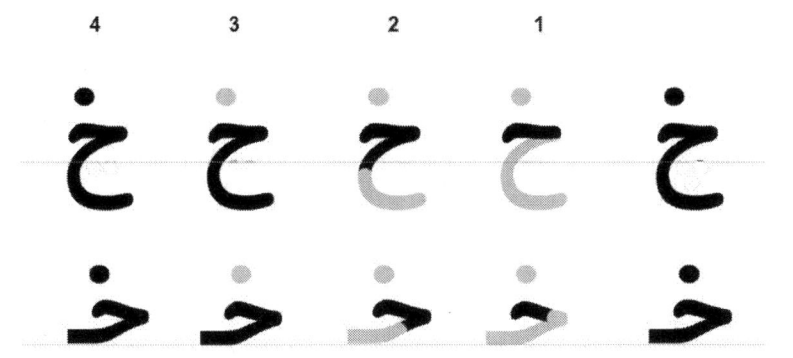

4   3   2   1

Sample Words

خواهَر sister :/khâhar/   خوابیدَن to sleep :/khâbidan/

تَخت bed, throne :/takht/   خوردَن to eat :/khordan/

خَسته tired :/khaste/   خانه house :/khâne/

Note: Sometimes the letter "و" is not pronounced in the words. For example, in words "خواهَر" and "خوابیدَن".

Sample Sentences

او تَخت دارَد.

ما خانه داریم.

او خَسته اَست.

Exercise: Practice the letters.

خِ : خِ – خِ – خِ – خِ – خِ – خِ – خِ – خِ

خِ – خِ – خِ – خِ – خِ – خِ – خِ – خِ – خِ

خَ : خَ – خَ – خَ – خَ – خَ – خَ – خَ – خَ – خَ

خَ – خَ – خَ – خَ – خَ – خَ – خَ – خَ – خَ – خَ

Improve Your Writing: Write on the sample words.

باخت: باخت – باخت – باخت – باخت

باخت – باخت – باخت – باخت

تخت: تَخْت – تَخْت – تَخْت – تَخْت

تَخْت – تَخْت – تَخْت – تَخْت – تَخْت

تاخت: تاخْت – تاخْت – تاخْت

تاخْت – تاخْت – تاخْت – تاخْت

Grammar Lesson

Simple Present of "to be"

هَستَم /hastam/: I am

هَستی /hasti/: You are (singular)

اَست – هَست /ast/–/hast/: He / She is

هَستیم /hastim/: We are

هَستید /hastid/: You (plural) are

هَستَند /hastand/: They are

Examples:

آنها هُنَرمَند هَستَند.

تو خَسته هَستی.

Grammar Lesson

Negative form of "to be"

More changes are required to make negative verbs for "to be".

I am not :/nistam/ نیستَم

You are (singular) not :/niasti/ نیستی

He / She is not :/nist/ نیست

We are not :/nistim/ نیستیم

You (plural) are not :/nistid/ نیستید

They are not :/nistand/ نیستَند

Examples:

آنها هُنَرمَند نیستَند.

تو خَسته نیستی.

ش – شـ

Name: "ش – شـ" called "shin", is the sixteenth letter of the Persian alphabet.

Sound: "ش" sounds /she/ like "sh" in "short".

Form: It has short and full formats.

How to write it

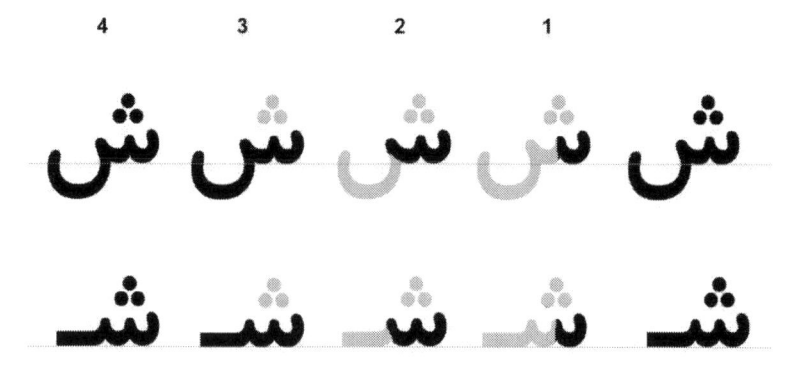

Sample Words

night :/shab/ شَب

swimming :/shenâ/ شنا

happy :/shâd/ شاد

to listen :/shenidan/ شِنیدَن

six :/shesh/ شِش

physician :/pezeshk/ پِزِشک

Sample Sentences

مَن پِزِشک هَستَم.

او شاد اَست.

مَن شِش کِتاب دارَم.

Exercise: Practice the letters.

شـ: شـ – شـ – شـ – شـ – شـ – شـ – شـ – شـ – شـ

شـ – شـ – شـ – شـ – شـ – شـ – شـ – شـ – شـ

ش: ش – ش – ش – ش – ش – ش – ش

ش – ش – ش – ش – ش – ش – ش

Improve Your Writing: Write on the sample words.

شش: شش – شش – شش – شش – شش

شش – شش – شش – شش – شش

شاد: شاد – شاد – شاد – شاد – شاد

شاد – شاد – شاد – شاد – شاد

شب: شب – شب – شب – شب – شب

شب – شب – شب – شب – شب

ف - فـ

Name: "ف - فـ" /fe/ is the twenty-third letter of the Persian alphabet.

Sound: "ف" sounds /fe/ like "f" in "film".

Form: It has two forms, short and full.

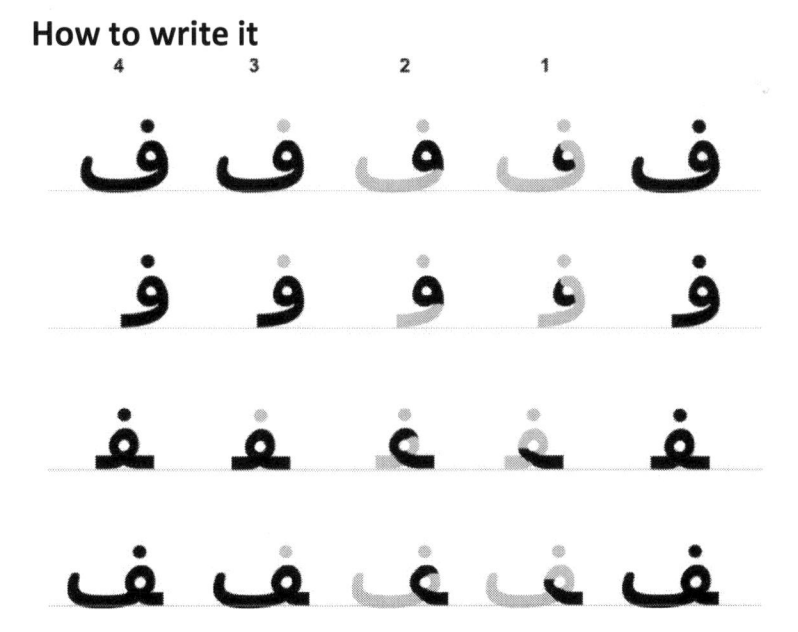

How to write it

Sample Words

فُروشَنده /forushande/: salesman

فَردا /fardâ/: tomorrow

فِرِستادَن /ferestâdan/: to send

فَرش /farsh/: carpet

فَهمیدَن /fahmidan/: to realize

فُروخـتَن /forukhtan/: to sell

Sample Sentences

فَردا هَوا خوب اَست.

او فُروشَندِه اَست.

تو یِک فَرش دارَی.

Exercise: Practice the letters.

ف: فـ – فـ – فـ – فـ – فـ – فـ – فـ – فـ

ف: ف – ف – ف – ف – ف – ف – ف – ف

Improve Your Writing: Write on the sample words

فرد: فرد – فرد – فرد – فرد – فرد – فرد

فرد – فرد – فرد – فرد – فرد – فرد

سفت: سفت – سفت – سفت – سفت – سفت

سفت – سفت – سفت – سفت – سفت

فردا: فردا – فردا – فردا – فردا – فردا

فردا – فردا – فردا – فردا – فردا

گ - گ

Name: "گ - گ" called "gâf", is the twenty-sixth letter of the Persian alphabet.

Sound: "گ" sounds /ge/ like "g" in "get".

Form: It has short and full forms.

How to write it

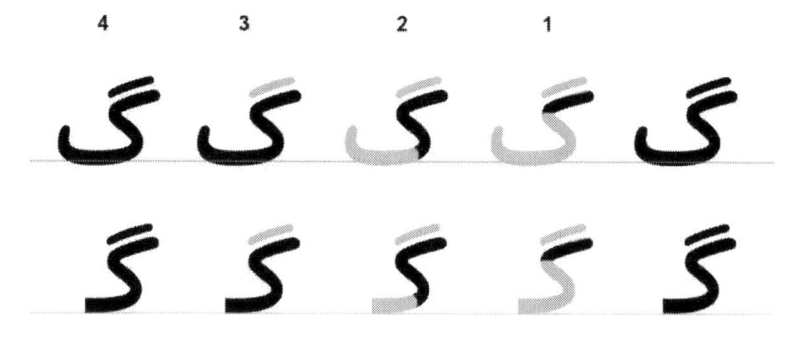

Sample Words

گُرُسنه /gorosne/: hungry   سَگ /sag/: dog

بَرگَشتَن /bargashtan/: to return   گاو /gâv/: cow

بُزُرگ /bozorg/: big   گُرگ /gorg/: wolf

Sample Sentences:

سارا سَگ دارَد.

آنها گاو دارَند.

سارا گُرُسنه اَست.

Exercise: Practice the letters.

گ: گ - گ - گ - گ - گ - گ - گ - گ

گ - گ - گ - گ - گ - گ - گ - گ

گ: گ - گ - گ - گ - گ - گ - گ - گ

گ - گ - گ - گ - گ - گ - گ - گ

Improve Your Writing: Write on the sample words.

گرگ: گرگ - گرگ - گرگ - گرگ - گرگ

گرگ - گرگ - گرگ - گرگ - گرگ

تگرگ: تگرگ - تگرگ - تگرگ - تگرگ

تگرگ - تگرگ - تگرگ - تگرگ

سگ: سگ - سگ - سگ - سگ - سگ

سگ - سگ - سگ - سگ - سگ

ق - ـق

Name: "ق - ـق" called "ghâf", is the twenty forth letter of the Persian alphabet.

Sound: "ق" sounds /ghe/ like "r" in French word "Paris", but it sounds stronger.

Form: It has short and full forms.

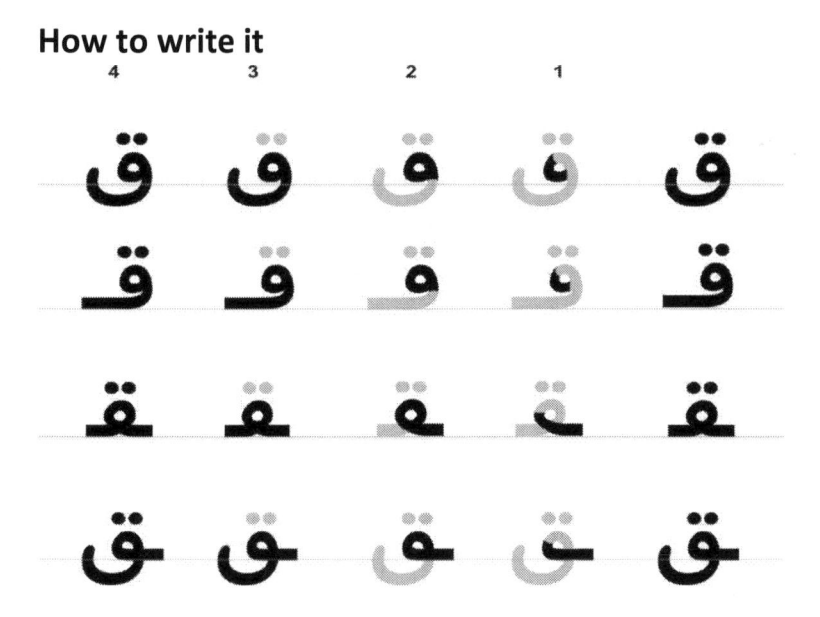

How to write it

Sample Words

قِیمَت /gheymat/: price   بُشقاب /boshghâb/: plate

قِیافه /ghiyâfe/: face, look   قاشُق /ghâshogh/: spoon

اُتاق /otâgh/: room   قَشَنگ /ghashang/: beautiful

Sample Sentences

سینا دَر اُتاق اَست.

این خانه قَشَنگ اَست.

خانه ما دو اُتاقِ بُزُرگ دارَد.

قِیمَتِ این بُشقاب خوب است.

Exercise: Practice the letters.

ق: قَ - قَ - قَ - قَ - قَ - قَ - قَ - قَ - قَ

ق: قُ - قُ - قُ - قُ - قُ - قُ - قُ - قُ - قُ

Improve Your Writing: Write on the sample words.

بشقاب: بشقاب - بشقاب - بشقاب - بشقاب

بشقاب - بشقاب - بشقاب - بشقاب

اُتاق: اُتاق - اُتاق - اُتاق - اُتاق - اُتاق

اُتاق - اُتاق - اُتاق - اُتاق

قَشَنگ: قَشَنگ - قَشَنگ - قَشَنگ - قَشَنگ

قَشَنگ - قَشَنگ - قَشَنگ - قَشَنگ

قیمَت: قیمَت - قیمَت - قیمَت - قیمَت

قیمَت - قیمَت - قیمَت - قیمَت - قیمَت

Grammar Lesson

Present Stem

This stem called "ستاکِ حال" /setâke hâl/ is used in shaping different forms of verbs including Present Continuous and Imperative verbs. The present steam in Persian is irregular.

ستاکِ حال Present Stem		
بین	To see	دیدَن
گو	To say	گُفتَن
نِویس	To write	نِوِشتَن
رو	To go	رَفتَن
آی	To come	آمَدَن

Present Verbal Endings

There are five Present Verbal Endings for six personal pronouns.

یم	ما /mâ/	م	من /man/
ید	شما /shomâ/	ی	تو /to/
ند	آنها - ایشان /ânhâ/ - /ishan/	...	او /u/

Present Progressive حالِ اخباری

I am saying.	می + گوی + م = می گویَم /miguyam/
S/he is going.	می + رو + د = می رَوَد /miravad/

87 www.LearnPersianOnline.com

We see.	می + بین + یم = می بینیم /mibinim/

Exercise 1: Join the letters and read the words:

۱. س + ت + ا + ر + ه

....

۲. م + د + ر + س + ه

....

۳. خ + س + ت + ه

....

۴. پ + ز + ش + ک

....

Exercise 2: Read the words and write in Persian.

1. Mehrabân...................

2. Ostâdân.....................

3. Khâne.......................

4. Takht........................

5. Shâd ....

6. Shenâ......................

7. Farsh......................

8. Gorg.......................

9. Ghashang................

10. gheimat.................

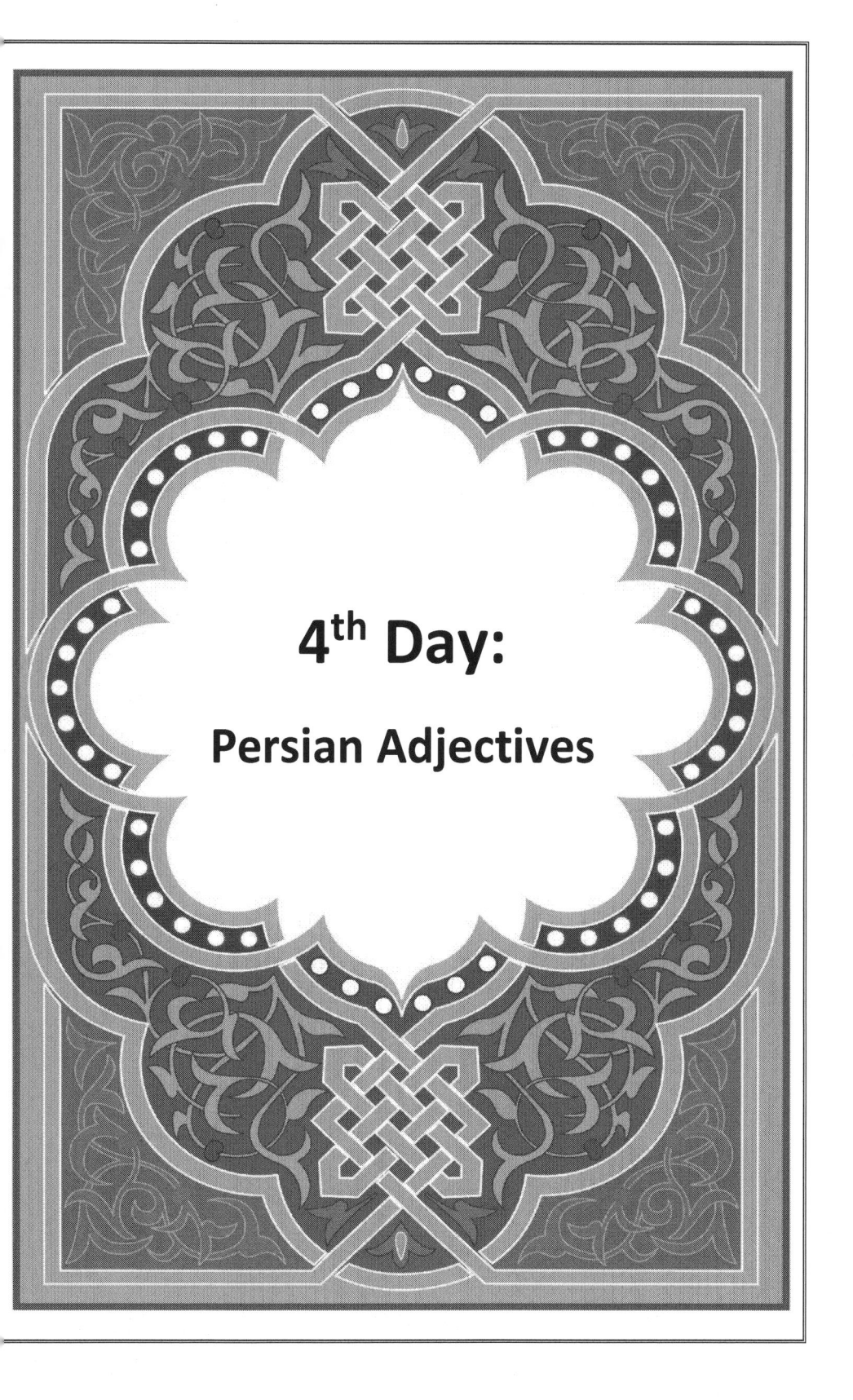

4th Day:

Persian Adjectives

ج - ج

Name: "ج - ج" /jim/ is the sixth letter of the Persian alphabet.

Sound: It sounds /je/ like "j" in "just".

Form: "ج" has short and full forms.

How to write it

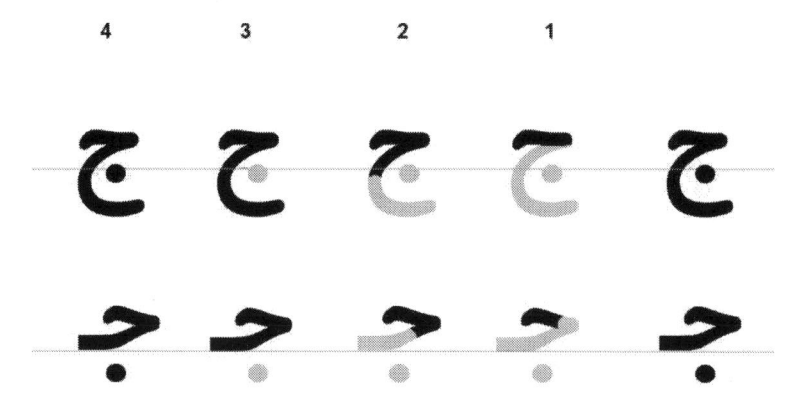

4   3   2   1

Sample Words

جوراب /jurab/: socks   تاج /tâj/: crown

جَشن /jashn/: ceremony   جادوگَر /jâdugar/: magician

جوجِه /juje/: chicken   جَواب /javâb/: reply

Sample Sentences

او تاج دارَد.

او بِه مَن جَواب داد.

او جوجِه دارَد.

Exercise: Practice the letters.

چ: چ - چ - چ - چ - چ - چ - چ - چ - چ

چ - چ - چ - چ - چ - چ - چ - چ - چ

ج: ج - ج - ج - ج - ج - ج - ج - ج - ج

ج - ج - ج - ج - ج - ج - ج - ج - ج

Improve Your Writing: Write on the sample words.

تاج: تاج - تاج - تاج - تاج - تاج - تاج

تاج - تاج - تاج - تاج - تاج - تاج

جار: جار - جار - جار - جار - جار - جار

جار - جار - جار - جار - جار - جار

جابجا: جابجا - جابجا - جابجا - جابجا - جابجا

جابجا - جابجا - جابجا - جابجا

Grammar Lesson

Adjectives

Adjectives usually follow the nouns to qualify them. Genitive حَرفِ اضافه or ی is used to connect nouns and adjectives.

شَهرِ بُزُرگ /shahre bozorg/: Big city

پسرهایِ خوب /pesarhâye khub/: Good boys

دُختَرِ زیبا /dokhtare zibâ/: Beautiful girl

دیوارِ بُلَند /divâre boland/: High wall

Genitive

Genitive sounds "e" as "e" in "men". It shows the possessive. Genitive is also used to connect two words.

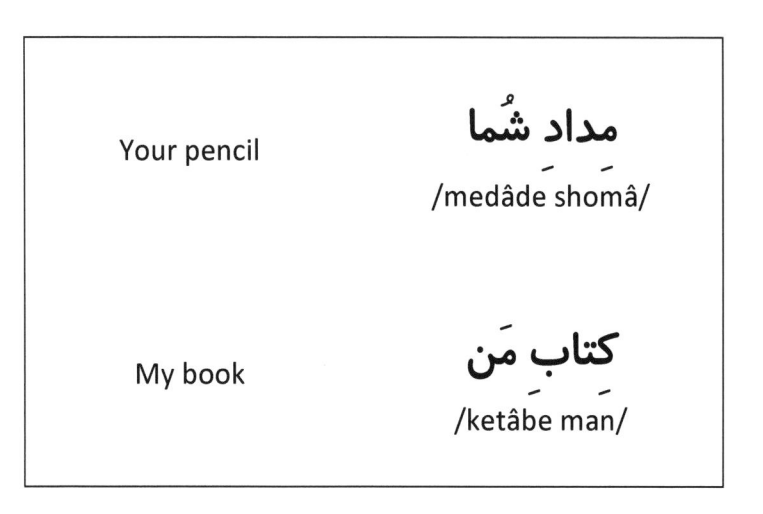

Your pencil	مِدادِ شُما /medâde shomâ/
My book	کِتابِ مَن /ketâbe man/

Genitive after vowels: "ی" is used as a genitive after vowels:

Our home	خانه‌ی ما /khâneye mâ/
Your school	مَدرِسه‌ی تو /madreseye to/

ل - ل

Name: "ل - ل" called "lâm", is the twenty-seventh letter of the Persian alphabet.

Sound: "ل" sounds /le/ like "l" in "leg".

Form: It has short and full forms.

How to write it

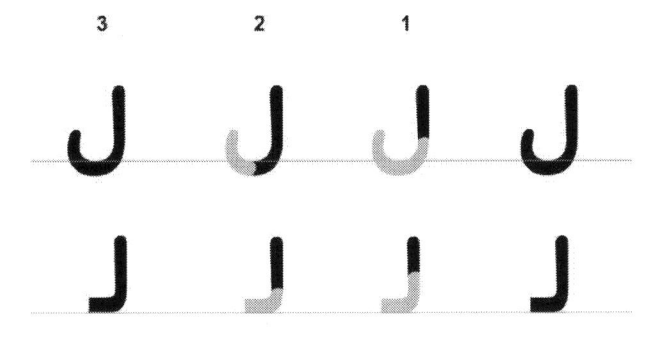

Sample Words

لِباس /lebâs/: dress　　　　　لَب /lab/: lip

گُلدان /goldân/: pot　　　　　لَک لَک /laklak/: stork

گُل /gol/: flower　　　　　کِلاس /kelâs/: class

Sample Sentences

لِباسِ سارا قَشَنگ اَست.

او بِه کِلاس می‌رَوَد.

این گُلها زیبا هَستَند.

Exercise: Practice the letters.

ل: ل - ل - ل - ل - ل - ل - ل - ل - ل - ل

ل - ل - ل - ل - ل - ل - ل - ل - ل - ل

ل: ل - ل - ل - ل - ل - ل - ل - ل - ل - ل

ل - ل - ل - ل - ل - ل - ل - ل - ل - ل

Improve Your Writing: Write on the sample words.

کلاس: کلاس - کلاس - کلاس - کلاس - کلاس

کلاس - کلاس - کلاس - کلاس - کلاس - کلاس

لک لک: لک لک - لک لک - لک لک - لک لک

لک لک - لک لک - لک لک - لک لک - لک لک

لب: لب - لب - لب - لب - لب - لب

لب - لب - لب - لب - لب - لب

چ - چ

Name: "چ - چ" /che/ is the seventh letter of the Persian alphabet.

Sound: It sounds /che/ like "ch" in "chair".

Form: Similar to "ج", it has short and full forms.

How to write it

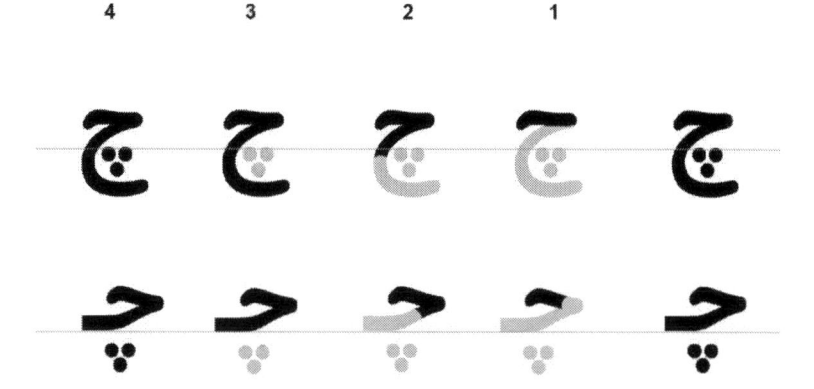

4   3   2   1

Sample Words

چَسباندَن /chasbândan/: to stick   چِهره /chehre/: visage, face

دوچَرخه /docharkhe/: bike   چَپ /chap/: left

چَشم /chashm/: eye   چیدَن /chidan/: to arrange

چَرب /charb/: oily

Sample Sentences

او دوچَرخه دارَد.

چَشمِ او سیاه[1] اَست.

---

[1] سیاه /siyâh/: black

Exercise: Practice the letters.

چ : جـ - جـ - جـ - جـ - جـ - جـ - جـ - جـ

جـ - جـ - جـ - جـ - جـ - جـ - جـ - جـ

ج : ج - ج - ج - ج - ج - ج - ج - ج - ج

ج - ج - ج - ج - ج - ج - ج - ج - ج

Improve Your Writing: Write on the sample words

چپ: چپ - چپ - چپ - چپ - چپ - چپ - چپ -

چپ - چپ - چپ - چپ - چپ - چپ - چپ

چرب: چرب - چرب - چرب - چرب - چرب -

چرب - چرب - چرب - چرب - چرب

چاپ: چاپ - چاپ - چاپ - چاپ - چاپ -

چاپ - چاپ - چاپ - چاپ - چاپ

ذ

Name: "ذ" called /zâl/, is the eleventh letter of the Persian alphabet.

Sound: It sounds /ze/ like "ze" in "zipper".

Form: It only has one format. "ذ" only joins to the preceding letters in Persian words.

How to write it

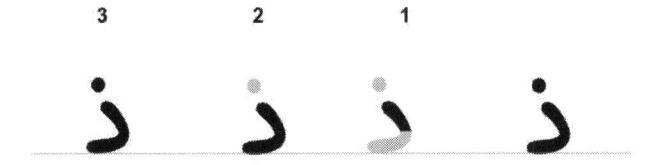

Sample Words

گُذاشتَن /gozâshtan/: to put   جَذاب /jazâb/: attractive

ذِهن /zehn/: mind   جَذب /jazb/: absorption

جاذِبه /jâzebe/: gravity   ذات /zât/: nature

اَذیَت /azyat/: tease

Sample Sentences:

سارا جَذاب اَست.

زَمین[1] جاذِبه دارَد.

---

[1] زَمین /zamin/: earth

Exercise: Practice the letters.

ذ: ذ – ذ – ذ – ذ – ذ – ذ – ذ – ذ – ذ – ذ

ذ – ذ – ذ – ذ – ذ – ذ – ذ – ذ – ذ – ذ

Improve Your Writing: Write on the sample words.

ذات: ذات – ذات – ذات – ذات – ذات – ذات

ذات – ذات – ذات – ذات – ذات – ذات

جذب: جذب – جذب – جذب – جذب –

جذب – جذب – جذب – جذب – جذب

جذاب: جذاب – جذاب – جذاب – جذاب –

جذاب – جذاب – جذاب – جذاب

Grammar lesson

Past Stem

This stem, called "ستاک گُذَشته" /setâke gozashte/, is used for writing different forms of verbs including simple past. The past stem is written similar to the infinitive without the letter "ن" at the end of it.

ستاکِ گذشته Past Stem		
دید	to see	دیدَن
گُفت	to say	گُفتَن
نوشت	to write	نوشتَن
رَفت	to go	رَفتَن
آمَد	to come	آمَدَن
شُست	to wash	شُستَن
نِشَست	to sit	نِشَستَن
خورد	to eat	خوردَن

Past Verbal Endings

There are five Past Verbal Endings for six personal pronouns:

م – ی – ... – یم – ید – ند

یم	ما /mâ/	م	مَن /man/
ید	شُما /shomâ/	ی	تو /to/
ند	آنها - ایشان /ânhâ/ - /ishan/	...	او /u/

Simple past of "to be"

بودَم /budam/: I was

بودی /budi/: You were (singular)

بود /bud/: He / She was

بودیم /budim/: We were

بودید /budid/: You (plural) were

بودَند /budand/: They were

Simple Past

مَن به مَدرِسه رَفتم.
/man be madrese raftam/

I went to school.

او یِک نامه نِوِشت.
/u yek nâme nevesht/

S/he wrote a letter.

صـ - ص

Name: "صـ – ص" called "sâd", is seventeenth letter of the Persian alphabet.

Sound: "ص" sounds /se/ like "s" in "sound".

Form: It has short and full forms.

How to write it

4   3   2   1

ص ص ص ص

صـ صـ صـ صـ

Sample Words

صورَت /surat/: face   صَبر /sabr/: patience

اِصابَت /esâbat/: strike   صَد /sad/: hundred

صَندَلی /sandali/: chair   صابون /sâbun/: soap

مَخصوص /makhsus/: special

Sample Sentences

او دَستِ خود[1] را[2] با صابون شُست.

مَن صورَتِ خود را شُستَم.

---

[1] خود /khod/: self

[2] object marker

Exercise: Practice the letters.

 صـ: صـ – صـ – صـ – صـ – صـ – صـ – صـ – صـ

صـ – صـ – صـ – صـ – صـ – صـ – صـ – صـ

ص: ص – ص – ص – ص – ص – ص – ص – ص

ص – ص – ص – ص – ص – ص – ص – ص

Improve Your Writing: Write on the sample words.

صبر: صبر – صبر – صبر – صبر – صبر

صبر – صبر – صبر – صبر – صبر

اصابت: اصابت – اصابت – اصابت – اصابت

اصابت – اصابت – اصابت – اصابت – اصابت

صد: صد – صد – صد – صد – صد – صد

صد – صد – صد – صد – صد – صد

ح - ﻫ

Name: "ﻫ - ح" /he/ is the eighth letter of the Persian alphabet.

Sound: It sounds /he/ like "h" in "his".

Form: "ح" has two forms, short and full.

How to write it

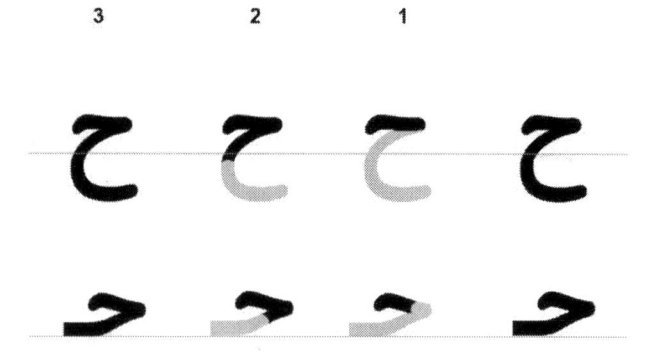

3   2   1

Sample Words

حاضِر /hâzer/: present   حُباب /hobâb/: bubble

حِجاب /hejâb/: veil   صُبح /sobh/: morning

حاجَت /hâjat/: need   صُبحانه /sobhâne/: breakfast

حوله /hôle/: towel

Sample Sentences

او صُبحِ زود بیدار می‌شَوَد.[1]

مَن صُبحانه خوردَم.

او حوله دارَد.

---

[1] he wakes up early in the morning

Exercise: Practice the letters.

ح : حـ - حـ - حـ - حـ - حـ - حـ - حـ

حـ - حـ - حـ - حـ - حـ - حـ - حـ

ج: ج - ج - ج - ج - ج - ج - ج - ج - ج

ج - ج - ج - ج - ج - ج - ج - ج - ج

Improve Your Writing: Write on the sample words

حباب: حباب - حباب - حباب - حباب

حباب - حباب - حباب - حباب - حباب

حجاب: حجاب - حجاب - حجاب - حجاب

حجاب - حجاب - حجاب - حجاب - حجاب

حاجت: حاجت - حاجت - حاجت - حاجت

حاجت - حاجت - حاجت - حاجت - حاجت

Exercise 1: Join the letters and read the words:

١. ج + و + ج + ه

....

٢. ل + ب + ا + س

....

٣. ک + ل + ا + س

....

۴. ص + و + ر + ت

....

Exercise 2: Read the words and write in Persian.

1. Juje....................

6. Zehn........................

2. Goldân......................

7. Sâbun........................

3. Lab........................

8. Hole........................

4. Chashm.......................

9. Sobh................

5. Chehre....................

10. hâjat................

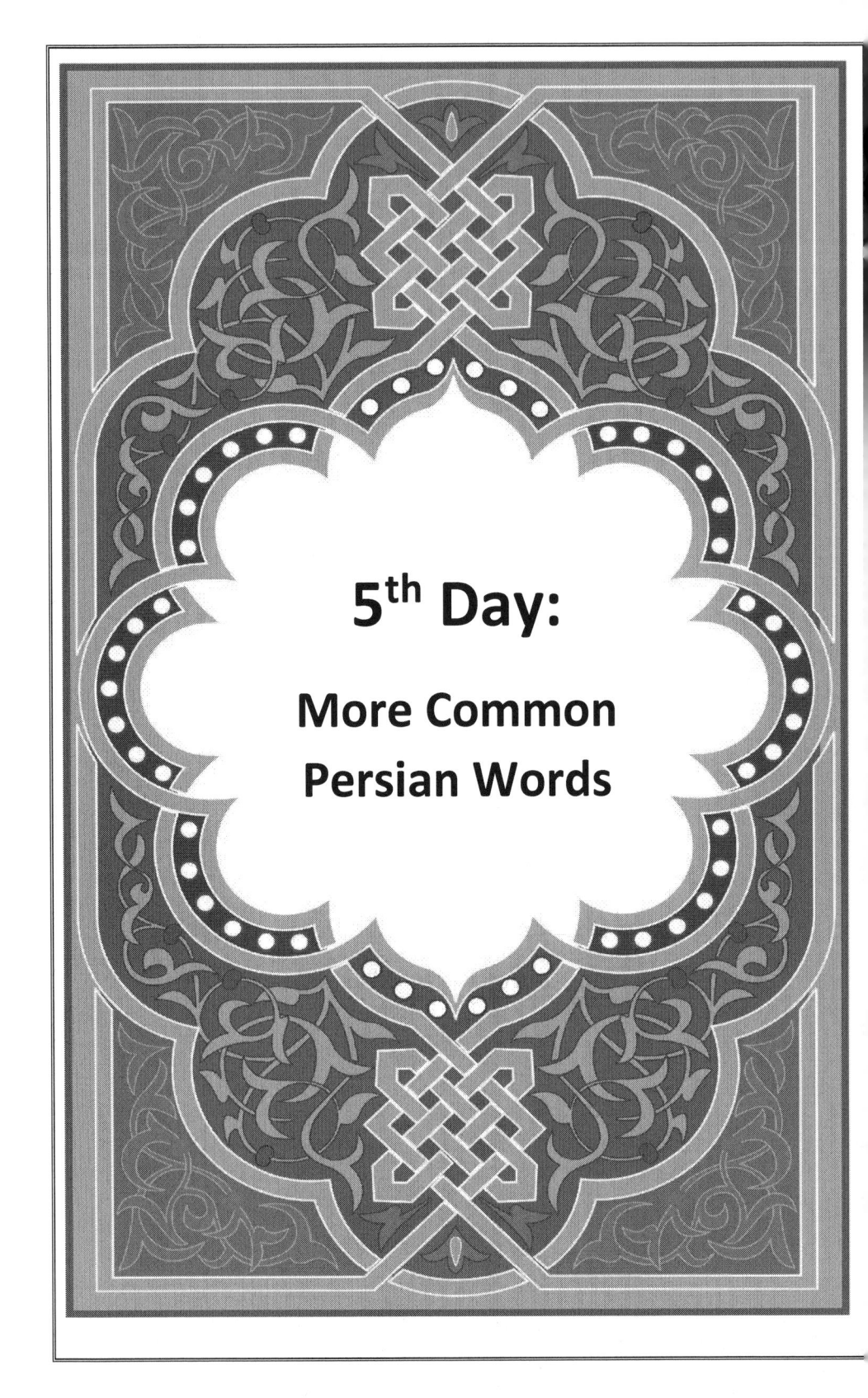

5th Day:

More Common Persian Words

ط

Name: "ط" called "tâ" is the nineteenth letter of the Persian alphabet.

Sound: "ط" sounds /te/ like "t" in "tablet".

Form: It only has one form and joins to the preceding and following letters in Persian words.

How to write it

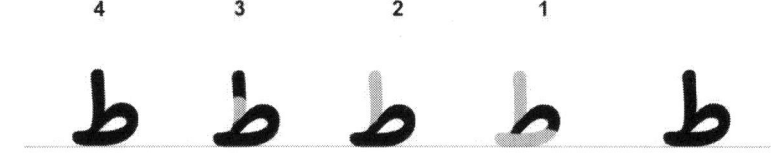

Sample Words

حَیاط /hayât/: yard طَرح /tarh/: plan

طَناب /tanâb/: rope اخطار /ekhtâr/: warning

طوفان /tufân/: flood خَطَر /khatar/: danger

Sample Sentences

بَچه ها دَر حَیاط بازی می کُنَند.^۱

آنها طَناب دارَند.

او طَرحِ خانه را کِشید.^۲

---

[1] children are playing in the yard.
[2] he drew a house layout.

Exercise: Practice the letters.

ط: ط – ط – ط – ط – ط – ط – ط – ط – ط

ط – ط – ط – ط – ط – ط – ط – ط – ط

Improve Your Writing: Write on the sample words.

خطر: خطر – خطر – خطر – خطر – خطر

خطر – خطر – خطر – خطر – خطر

اخطار: اخطار – اخطار – اخطار – اخطار

اخطار – اخطار – اخطار – اخطار – اخطار

طرح: طرح – طرح – طرح – طرح – طرح

طرح – طرح – طرح – طرح – طرح – طرح

ع - ـع

Name: "ع - ـع" called "eyn", is the twenty-first letter of the Persian alphabet.

Form: It has short and full forms. "ع" is written in four ways:

Initial letter:	عَدَد	/adad/	Number
Medial letter:	جُمعه	/jom'e/	Friday
Final joined Letter:	طَبع	/tab'/	Nature
Final disjoined letter:	شُروع	/shoru'/	Start

How to write it

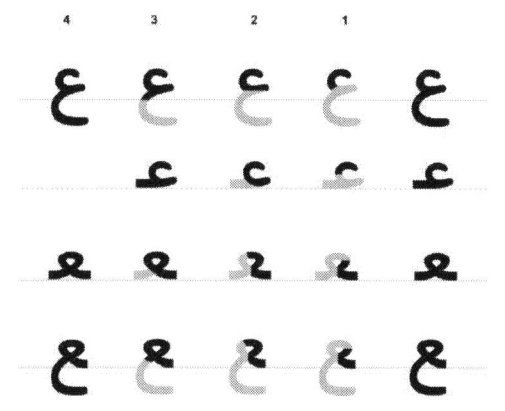

4	3	2	1
ع	ع	ع	ع
ـع	ـع	ـع	ـع
ـعـ	ـعـ	ـعـ	ـعـ
عـ	عـ	عـ	عـ

Sample Words

ساعَت /sâ'at/: hour   ساعد /sâed/: forearm

جَمع /jam'/: total   سعی /sa'y/: effort

موقِع /moghe'/: time   عَرَب /arab/: Arab

Sample Sentences

اِمروز جُمعه اَست.

سارا بِه خانه‌ی عَمو¹ رَفت.

آن ساعَت اَست.

Exercise: Practice the letters.

عـ: عـ – عـ – عـ – عـ – عـ – عـ – عـ – عـ – عـ

ع: ع – ع – ع – ع – ع – ع – ع – ع – ع

Improve Your Writing: Write on the sample words.

عرب: عرب – عرب – عرب – عرب – عرب

سعی: سعی – سعی – سعی – سعی – سعی

ساعد: ساعد – ساعد – ساعد – ساعد – ساعد

---

[1] uncle

ظ

Name: "ظ" called "zâ" is the twentieth letter of the Persian alphabet.

Sound: "ظ" sounds /ze/ like "z" in "zipper".

Form: It only has one form and joins to the preceding and following letters in Persian words.

How to write it

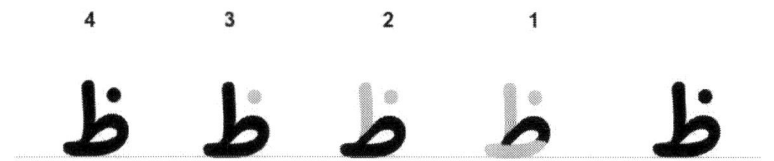

| 4 | 3 | 2 | 1 |

Sample Words

خُداحافِظی /khodâhâfezi/:
goodbye

ظالِم /zâlem/: cruel

ظُهر /zohr/: noon

ظَرف /zarf/: dish

ظاهِر /zâher/: appearance

حِفظ /hefz/: protect

Sample Sentences

او ظُهر بِه خانه آمَد.

مادَرَم ظَرفها را شُست.[1]

---

[1] my mother washed the dishes.

Exercise: Practice the letters.

ظ: ظ – ظ – ظ – ظ – ظ – ظ – ظ – ظ – ظ

ظ – ظ – ظ – ظ – ظ – ظ – ظ – ظ – ظ

Improve Your Writing: Write on the sample words.

حفظ: حفظ – حفظ – حفظ – حفظ – حفظ – حفظ

حفظ – حفظ – حفظ – حفظ – حفظ – حفظ

ظرف: ظرف – ظرف – ظرف – ظرف

ظرف – ظرف – ظرف – ظرف – ظرف

ظالم: ظالم – ظالم – ظالم – ظالم – ظالم

ظالم – ظالم – ظالم – ظالم – ظالم

ث - ثـ

Name: "ثـ - ث" /se/ is the fifth letter of the Persian alphabet.

Sound: "ث" sounds /se/ like "s" in "Second".

Form: It has short and full forms.

How to write it

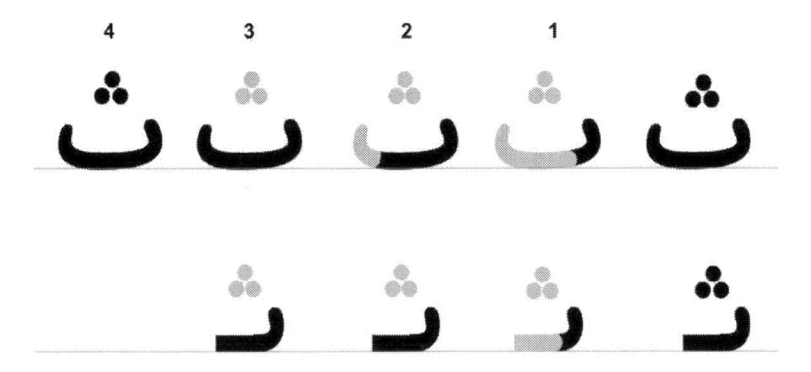

Sample Words

مُثبَت /mosbat/: positive

ثابِت /sabet/: stable

مِثال /mesâl/: example

ثَبت /sabt/: registration

ثِروَت /servat/: wealth

اَثاث /asâs/: furniture

مُثَلَث /mosalas/: triangle

Sample Sentences

این مُثَلَث اَست.

او ثِروَتِ زیادی[1] دارَد.

---

[1] زیاد /ziyâd/: much, many

Exercise: Practice the letters.

ثـ : ثـ – ثـ – ثـ – ثـ – ثـ – ثـ – ثـ – ثـ – ثـ

ثـ – ثـ – ثـ – ثـ – ثـ – ثـ – ثـ – ثـ – ثـ

ث: ث – ث – ث – ث – ث – ث – ث – ث

ث – ث – ث – ث – ث – ث – ث – ث

Improve Your Writing: Write on the sample words.

ثبت: ثبت – ثبت – ثبت – ثبت – ثبت – ثبت

ثبت – ثبت – ثبت – ثبت – ثبت – ثبت – ثبت

ثابت: ثابت – ثابت – ثابت – ثابت – ثابت – ثابت

ثابت – ثابت – ثابت – ثابت – ثابت – ثابت

اثاث: اثاث – اثاث – اثاث – اثاث – اثاث – اثاث

اثاث – اثاث – اثاث – اثاث – اثاث – اثاث

ض - ضـ

Name: "ض" called "zâd", is the eighteenth letter of the Persian alphabet.

Sound: "ض" sounds /ze/ like "z" in "zipper".

Form: It has short and full forms.

How to write it

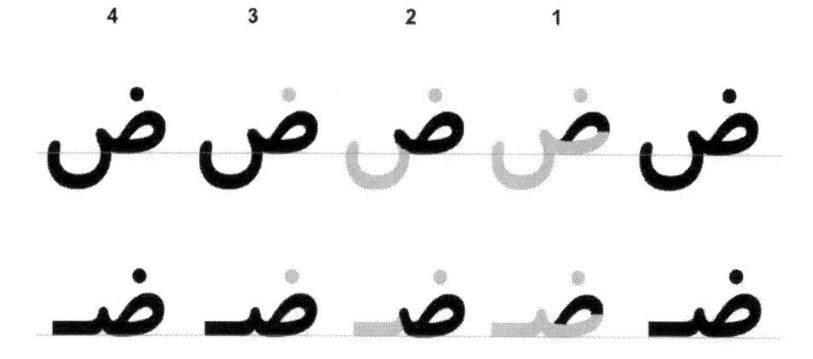

Sample Words

مَریض /mariz/: patient   ضَرَر /zarar/: damage

حاضِر /hâzer/: present   ضارِب /zâreb/: assailant

بَعضی /ba'zi/: some   ضَربه /zarbe/: impact

Sample Sentences

او مَریض اَست.

ناهار[1] حاضر بود.

---

[1] ناهار /nâhâr/: lunch

Exercise: Practice the letters.

ضـ: ضـ – ضـ – ضـ – ضـ – ضـ – ضـ – ضـ

ضـ – ضـ – ضـ – ضـ – ضـ – ضـ – ضـ

ض: ض – ض – ض – ض – ض – ض – ض

ض – ض – ض – ض – ض – ض – ض

Improve Your Writing: Write on the sample words.

ضربه: ضربه – ضربه – ضربه – ضربه

ضربه – ضربه – ضربه – ضربه

ضارب: ضارب – ضارب – ضارب – ضارب

ضارب – ضارب – ضارب – ضارب

ضرر: ضرر – ضرر – ضرر – ضرر – ضرر

ضرر – ضرر – ضرر – ضرر – ضرر – ضرر

غ - غـ

Name: "غ - غـ" called "gheyn" is the twenty-second letter of the Persian alphabet.

Sound: "غ" sounds /ghe/ like "r" in French word "Paris", but "غ" is stronger.

Form: It has short and full forms.
"غ" is written in four ways:

Initial letter: غریب /gharib/ Strange

Medial letter: مشغول /mashghul/ Busy

Final joined Letter: جیغ /jigh/ Scream

Final disjoined letter: باغ /bâgh/ Garden

How to write it

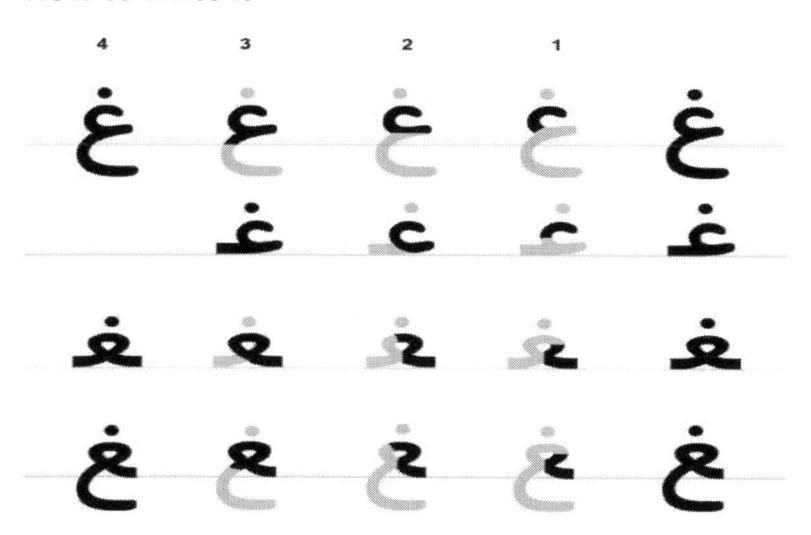

Sample Words

garden :/bâgh/ باغ

hot :/dâgh/ داغ

scream :/jigh/ جیغ

west :/gharb/ غَرب

blade :/tigh/ تیغ

dense :/ghaliz/ غَلیظ

gardener :/bâghebân/ باغِبان

busy :/mashghul/ مَشغول

Sample Sentences

آنها به باغ رَفتَند.

سوپ' خِیلی غَلیظ بود.

Exercise: Practice the letters.

غـ: غـ - غـ - غـ - غـ - غـ - غـ - غـ - غـ - غـ

غ: غ - غ - غ - غ - غ - غ - غ - غ - غ

Improve Your Writing: Write on the sample words.

غلیظ: غلیظ - غلیظ - غلیظ - غلیظ - غلیظ - غلیظ

غرب: غرب - غرب - غرب - غرب - غرب - غرب

داغ: داغ - داغ - داغ - داغ - داغ - داغ

---

[1] سوپ /sup/: soup

ژ

Name: "ژ" /zhe/ is the fourteenth letter of the Persian alphabet

Sound: It has one form. "ژ" only joins to the preceding letters in Persian words.

Form: It sounds /zhe/ like "su" in "measure".

How to write it

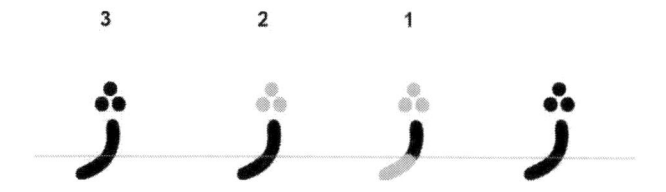

Sample Words

پَژوهِش /pazhuhesh/: research   دِژ /dezh/: castle

ژولیده /zhulideh/: slovenly   ژاکَت /zhâkat/: jacket

ژِست /zhest/: gesture

Sample Sentences

او یِک ژاکَت خَرید.

آن دِژ قَدیمی اَست.

ژِستِ او جالِب بود.

موهایَت ژولیده است.

Exercise: Practice the letters.

ژ: ژ – ژ – ژ – ژ – ژ – ژ – ژ – ژ – ژ – ژ

ژ – ژ – ژ – ژ – ژ – ژ – ژ – ژ – ژ – ژ

Improve Your Writing: Write on the sample words.

دژ: دژ – دژ – دژ – دژ – دژ – دژ – دژ – دژ

دژ – دژ – دژ – دژ – دژ – دژ – دژ – دژ

ژست: ژست – ژست – ژست – ژست

ژست – ژست – ژست – ژست – ژست

ژاکت: ژاکت – ژاکت – ژاکت – ژاکت

ژاکت – ژاکت – ژاکت – ژاکت – ژاکت

Grammar Lesson

Question Words

Question words appear in the beginning or middle of the sentence.

کُجا /kojâ/: Where

کی (چِه کَسی) /ki (che kasi)/: Who

کِی /key/: When

چِه /che/: What

چی /chi/: What

چِطُور /chetor/: How

چَند /chand/: How many

Exercise 1: Join the letters and read the words:

١. ج + و + ج + ه

....

٢. ل + ب + ا + س

....

٣. ک + ل + ا + س

....

۴. ص + و + ر + ت

....

Exercise 2: Read the words and write in Persian.

1. tanâb........................

2. khatar......................

3. adad.........................

4. sâed.........................

5. hefz..........................

6. zâher........................

7. mosalas....................

8. hazer........................

9. bâgh.........................

10. chetor.....................

6th Day:

Let's Count in Persian

Numbers

Numbers are written from left to write in Persian:

1   ۱   یک /yek/

2   ۲   دُو /do/

3   ۳   سه /se/

4   ۴   چِهار /chehâr/

5   ۵   پَنج /panj/

6	۶	شِش /shesh/
7	۷	هَفت /haft/
8	۸	هَشت /hasht/
9	۹	نه /noh/
10	۱۰	دَه /dah/

Mathematical symbols   عَلامَت هایِ ریاضی

÷   ×   =   −   +

تَقسیم   ضَرب   مُساوی   مِنها   جَمع

Division   Multiplication   Equal   Subtraction   Addition

Practice 1: Write in letters.

a) ۴ ....

b) ۶ ....

c) ۹ ....

d) ۷ ....

e) ۸ ....

f) ۳ ....

g) ۱ ....

h) ۵ ....

Practice 2: Write the answers in letters.

a) ۱+ ۲ = ...

b) ۳ – ۹ = ...

c) ۲ + ۲ = ...

d) ۳ - ۵ = ...

e) ۱ + ۸ = ...

f) ۴ - ۷ = ...

10	۱۰	/dah/	دَه
20	۲۰	/bist/	بیست
30	۳۰	/si/	سی
40	۴۰	/chehel/	چِهِل
50	۵۰	/panjâh/	پنجاه
60	۶۰	/shast/	شَصت
70	۷۰	/haftâd/	هفتاد
80	۸۰	/hastâd/	هشتاد
90	۹۰	/navad/	نَوَد
100	۱۰۰	/sad/	صَد

200	۲۰۰	/devist/	**دِویست**
300	۳۰۰	/sisat/	**سیصَد**
400	۴۰۰	/chehârsad/	**چِهارصَد**
500	۵۰۰	/pânsad/	**پانصَد**
600	۶۰۰	/sheshsad/	**شِشصَد**
700	۷۰۰	/haftsad/	**هَفتصَد**
800	۸۰۰	/hashtsad/	**هَشتصَد**
900	۹۰۰	/nohsad/	**نُهصَد**
1000	۱۰۰۰	/hezâr/	**هِزار**

Practice 3: Write in letters.

a) ۱۲ ....

b) ۱۴ ....

c) ۱۷ ....

d) ۱۹ ....

e) ۱۵ ....

f) ۱۳ ....

g) ۱۶ ....

h) ۲۰ ....

i) ۱۰۰ ....

j) ۸۰۰ ....

Practice 4: Write the answers in letters.

a) ۳۰ + ۶۰ ....

b) ۴۰ + ۳۰ ....

c) ۳۰ + ۵۰ ....

d) ۵۰ + ۴۰ ....

e) ۱۰ + ۹۰ ....

f) ۱۰۰ + ۸۰۰ ....

g) ۲۰۰ + ۳۰۰ ....

h) ۸۰۰۰ + ۶۰۰۰ + ۱۰۰ ....

Arabic signs in Persian

Three Arabic signs are used in Persian.

1- " ّ " is called "tashdid" (in Arabic is called "Shadda") and it indicates a doubling of the preceding consonant. In many Persian text books, tashdid is not written and pronounced.

Sample Words:

- مُحَمَّد /mohammad/: common name
- بَچَّه /bache/: child
- بَرَّه /bare/: lamb

2- " اً " is called "tanvin" (in Arabic "Tanwiin") and is

a grammatical suffix (an "attachment" to the end of the word). Tanvin sounds "an" and it always come at the end of Arabic words that are used in Persian.

Sample Words:

- كاملاً /kâmelan/: completely
- مَثَلاً /masalan/: for example
- دَقيقاً /daghighan/: exactly

3- "أ" is called "Hamze" (in Arabic "Hamza") and sounds the glottal stop. Its sound is similar to letter "ع". Hamze is written in four forms: "ء" "ئـ", "أ" and "ؤ".

Sample Words:

- پائیز /pâiz/: the autumn
- شیء /she'y/: object
- تأثیر /ta'sir/: effect, impact
- امضاء /emza'/: signature

7th Day:

Time to Read in Persian

Text 1   مَتن ۱

سینا وَ سارا با پِدَر وَ مادَر بِه باغ رَفتَند.

باغِبان با پِدَرِ آنها دوست بود.

باغِبان مَشغولِ کار بود.

باغِبان بَرایِ آنها گُل چید[1].

ساقِهِ‌یِ گُل[2] پُر اَز خار بود.

---

[1] to pick
[2] peddicel

Text 2

مَتن ۲

کامران وَ ثُرَیا بِه مَدرِسه می‌رَوَند.

ثُرَیا مِثلِ[1] سارا شاگِردِ[2] مُمتاز[3] اَست.

کامران وَ سینا هَمکلاسی[4] هَستَند.

ثُرَیا وَ سارا هَمکلاسی هَستَند.

---

[1] like
[2] student
[3] elect
[4] classmate

Text 3   مَتن ۳

سارا وَ مَهدیس دُختَر عَمو[1] هَستَند.

روزِ جُمعه سارا به خانه‌ی عَمو[2] رَفت.

سارا وَ مَهدیس با هَم بازی کَردَند[3].

آنها موقعِ ناهار بازی را تَمام کَردَند[4].

---

[1] cousin
[2] uncle
[3] to playing
[4] to finish

Text 4   مَتن ۴

سینا وَ سارا صُبح زود اَز خواب بیدار می‌شَوَند.

آنها هَر روز صُبح دَست و صورتِ خود را با صابون می‌شویَند.

آنها دَست و صورتِ خود را با حوله خُشک می‌کُنَند.

آنها با پِدَر وَ مادَر صُبحانه می‌خورَند.

Text 5 مَتن ۵

سارا با مادَرِ به بازار رَفت.

آنها دَر بازار خَرید کَردَند[1].

سارا لِباس خَرید.

مادَر بِه فُرُوشَندهِ[2] پول داد.

لِباسِ سارا یک پیراهَن اَست.

پیراهَنِ سارا گُلهایِ قَشَنگی دارَد.

---
[1] to buy
[2] seller

Text 6   مَتن ۶

اِمروز باران بارید[1].

اِمروز باران تُند بارید.

مَن اِمروز بیرون بودَم.

مَن وَ سارا اِمروز بیرون بودیم.

---

[1] to rain

Text 7   مَتن ۷

سینا سه روز بیمار بود.

سینا به مدرسه می‌رود.

مادر سینا به مدیر نامه[1] می‌نویسد.

او می‌نویسد سینا سه روز بیمار بود.

---

[1] letter

Days of the week: روزهایِ هَفته /ruzhâye hafte/

Saturday	/shanbe/	شَنبه
Sunday	/yekshanbe/	یکشَنبه
Monday	/doshanbe/	دوشَنبه
Tuesday	/seshanbe/	سه شَنبه
Wednesday	/chehârshanbe/	چهارشَنبه
Thursday	/panjshanbe/	پَنج شَنبه
Friday	/Jom'e/	جُمعه

شَنبه روزِ اَول[1] هَفته اَست.

Saturday is the first day of the week.

جُمعه روزِ آخَر[2] هَفته اَست.

Friday is the last day of the week.

جُمعه دَر ایران تَعطیل[3] اَست.

Friday is a holiday in Iran.

---

[1] first
[2] last
[3] holiday

Example:

امروز چَند شَنبه است؟

/emruz chand shanbe ast?/

What day is today?

فَردا چَند شَنبه اَست؟

/farad chand shanbe ast?/

What day will it be tomorrow?

چَند شَنبه تَعطیل اَست؟

/chand shanbe ta'til ast/

What day is holiday?

امروز سه شَنبه اَست.

/emruz seshanbe ast/

Today is Tuesday.

فَردا چهارشَنبه اَست.

/farad chehârshanbe ast/

Tomorrow will be Wednesday.

جُمعه تَعطیل اَست.

/jom'e ta'til ast/

Friday is holiday.

Most common persian phrases

سَلام: Hello

/salām/

حالِ شُما چِطورِه؟: How are you?

/hāle shomā chetore?/

مَن خوبَم شُما چِطورید؟: I'm fine, and you?

/man khoobam shomā chetorid?/

چه خَبَر؟: What's up?

/che khabar?/

صُبح بِخیر: Good morning

/sobh Be kheyr/

Good evening :عَصر بِخیر

/asr be kheyr/

Thank you (very much) :مِرسی

/mersi/

You're welcome! (for "thank you") :خواهِش می‌کُنَم

/khāhesh mikonam/

Welcome! (to greet someone) :خوش آمَدید

/khosh āmadid/

Good night :شَب بِخیر

/shab be kheyr/

خُداحافظ: Good bye

/khodahāfez/

اِسمِ شُما چیه؟ What's your name?

/esme shomā chiye?/

اِسمِ مَن جیسون اَست: My name is Jason

/esme man jason hast/

اَز دیدَنِ شُما خوشبَختَم. Nice to meet you!

/az didane shomā khoshbakhtam/

شُما اَهلِ کُجا هَستید؟ Where are you from?

/shoma ahleh kojā hastid?/

مَن اَهلِ ایران هَستَم. I'm from Iran.

/man ahle irānam/

چَند سالَت اَست؟ How old are you?

/chand sālet ast?/

مَن بیست سال دارَم. I'm twenty years old.

/man bist sāl dāram/

ساعَت چَنده؟ What time is it?

/sā'at chande?/

شُغلِ شُما چیه؟ What do you do?

/shoghle shomā chiye?/

روزِ خوبی داشتِه باشید. !Have a nice day

/rooze khobi dāshte bashed/

سال نو مبارک! !Happy new year

/sāle no mobārak/

تبریک میگویَم. !Congratulations

/tabrik miguyam/

ببخشید! Sorry! (for a mistake)

/bebakhshid/

قیمتش چنده؟ ?How much is this

/gheymatesh chande?/

پاسُخِ سوالات

Exercise Answers

1st Day

Exercise1:

۱. بَدَن

۲. باران

۳. بادام

۴. سَبَد

Exercise 2:

۶. مادَر ۱. نان

۷. نام ۲. بَد

۸. اَسب ۳. آنار

۹. سَگ ۴. مَرد

۱۰. آرد ۵. سَر

2nd Day

Exercise1:

١. دَست

٢. کارمَند

٣. بازار

۴. دوست

Exercise 2:

١. مَتن	۶. بیدار
٢. کِتاب	٧. توت
٣. کَم	٨. رود
۴. زبان	٩. پَرواز
۵. بیمار	١٠. پُر

3rd Day

Exercise1:

۱. سِتاره

۲. مَدرِسه

۳. خَسته

۴. پِزِشک

Exercise 2:

۶. شِنا

۷. فَرش

۸. گُرگ

۹. قَشَنگ

۱۰. قِیمَت

۱. مِهرَبان

۲. اُستادان

۳. خانه

۴. تَخت

۵. شاد

4th Day

Exercise1:

١. جادوگَر

٢. لِباس

٣. کِلاس

٤. صورَت

Exercise 2:

٦. ذِهن

٧. صابون

٨. حوله

٩. صُبح

١٠. حاجَت

١. جوجه

٢. گُلدان

٣. لَب

٤. چَشم

٥. چِهره

5th Day

Exercise1:

١. طوفان

٢. جُمعه

٣. ساعَت

٤. مُثبَت

Exercise 2:

١. طَناب	٦. ظاهِر
٢. خَطَر	٧. مُثَلَث
٣. عَدَد	٨. حاضِر
٤. ساعِد	٩. باغ
٥. حِفظ	١٠. چِطور

6th Day

Exercise 1:

a) چِهار

b) شِش

c) نُه

d) هَفت

e) هَشت

f) سه

g) یِک

h) پَنج

Exercise 2:

a) سه

b) شِش

c) چِهار

d) دو

e) نه

f) سه

Exercise 3:

a) دَوازدَه

b) چِهاردَه

c) هفدَه

d) نوزدَه

e) پانزدَه

f) سیزدَه

g) شانزدَه

h) بیست

i) صد

j) هشتصد

Exercise 4:

a) نَوَد

b) هَفتاد

c) هَشتاد

d) نَوَد

e) صَد

f) نُهصَد

g) پانصَد

h) هَفتصَد

واژِگان

Glossary

اَصلی /asli/: primary	آب /âb/: water
اَما /amâ/: but	اُتاق /otâgh/: room
آماده کَردَن /âmâde kardan/: to prepare	آتَش /âtash/: fire
آمَدَن /âmadan/: to come	اَثاث /asâs/: furniture
اِمروز /emruz/: today	آخَرین /âkharin/: last
آموختَن /âmukhtan/: to teach	اِخطار /ekhtâr/: alarm
آن /ân/: that- it	اِدامه یافتَن /edâme yâftan/: to continue
اَنار /anâr/: pomegranate	اَذیَت /azyat/: tease
اَنجام دادَن /anjâm dâdan/: to perform	آرد /ârd/: flour
اَنداختَن /andâkhtan/: to drop	اَرز /arz/: currency
اَنعام /an'âm/: tip	اَرزش /arzesh/: value
آنها /ânhâ/: they	آزار /âzâr/: hurt
او /u/: she – he	آزمون /âzmun/: test
آوَردَن /âvardan/: to bring	اَسب /asb/: horse
اوَلین /avalin/: first	اُستاد /ostâd/: teacher
ایرانی /irâni/: Iranian	اِسم /esm/: name
این /in/: this	آش /âsh/: pottage
	اِصابَت /esâbat/: strike

بَرای /barâye/: for	با /bâ/: with - by
بَرای اینکه /barâye inke/: because	بابا /bâbâ/: dad
بَرداشتَن /bardâshtan/: to pickup	باد /bâd/: wind
بُردَن /bordan/: to win – to take	بادام /bâdâm/: almonds
بَرگُزار کَردَن /bagozâr kardan/: to held up	بادِقَّت /bâ deghat/: careful
بُردَن /burden/: to carry	بار /bâr/: load
بَرگَشتَن /bargashtan/: to comeback	باران /bârân/: rain
بَرگه /barge/: paper	باز /bâz/: open
بِرِنج /berenj/: rice	بازار /bâzâr/: market
بُز /boz/: goat	بازی کَردَن /bâzi kardan/: to play
بُزُرگ /bozorg/: big - large	باعث /bâes/: cause
بَستَنی /bastani/: ice cream	باغ /bâgh/: garden
بِسیار /besyâr/: very	باغبان /bâghebân/: gardener
بُشقاب /boshghâb/: plate	بَچه /ba'che/: child
بَعد اَز /badaz/: after	بَخشیدَن /bakhshidan/: to forgive
بَعضی /ba'zi/: some	بَد /bad/: bad
بَند /band/: rope	بَدَن /badan/: body

پیراهَن /pirâhan/: shirt	بِه /be/: in - into
پیش /pish/: foreside - past	بِهتَر /behtar/: better
تاب /tâb/: swing	بودَن /budan/: to be
تاج /tâj/: crown	بیدار شدن / bidâr shodan/: to wake up
تَب /tab/: fever	
تَبَر /tabar/: chopper	بیرون /birun/: outside
تَپه /tape/: hill	بیشتَر /bishtar/: more
تَخت /takht/: bed - throne	پا /pâp/: foot - leg
ترجیح دادن /tarjih dâdan/: to prefer	پاپ /pâp/: the Pope
	پُختَن /pokhtan/: to cook
تَرس /tars/: fear	پدَر /pedar/: father
تَرسیدَن /tarsidan/: to scare	پُر /por/: full
تَعَجُب /ta'ajob/: surprise	پرَنده /parande/: bird
تَعطیل /ta'til/: holiday	پرواز /parvâz/: fly
تَفریح /tafrih/: recreation	پَریدَن /pardian/: to jump
تَقویم /taghvim/: calendar	پِسَر /pesar/: son - boy
تَلاش کَردَن /talâsh kardan/: to endeavor	پُشت /posht/: back
تلفُن /telefon/: telephone	پَهن /pahn/: wide
	پول /pul/: money

answer :/jurâb/ جَواب	clean :/tamiz/ تَمیز
chicken :/juje/ جوجه	lazy :/tanbal/ تَنبَل
socks :/jurab/ جوراب	you :/to/ تو
to chew :/javidan/ جویدَن	ball :/tup/ توپ
shout :/jigh/ جیغ	berry :/shâhtut/ توت
tea :/châi/ چای	stable :/sabet/ ثابِت
left :/chap/ چَپ	registration :/sabt/ ثَبت
to stick :/chasbândan/ چَسباندَن	wealth :/servat/ ثروَت
eye :/chashm/ چَشم	to move :/jâbejâ kardan/ جابه جا کَردَن
several :/chand/ چَند	mare :/jâdugar/ جادوگَر
whom - who :/che kasi/ چِه کَسی	breath :/jân/ جان
:/chehârshanbe/ چِهارشَنبِه Wednesday	modern :/jadid/ جَدید
face :/chehre/ چِهرِه	cute :/jazâb/ جَذاب
wood :/chub/ چوب	absorption :/jazb/ جَذب
to arrange :/chidan/ چیدَن	ceremony :/jashn/ جَشن
thing :/chiz/ چیز	addition :/jam'/ جَمع
need :/hâjat/ حاجَت	jangle - forest :/jangal/ جَنگَل
	world :/jahân/ جهان

sleep :/khâb/ خواب	present :/hâzer/ حاضر
resting :/khâbide/ خوابیده	bubble :/hobâb/ حُباب
sister :/khâhar/ خواهَر	veil :/hejâb/ حِجاب
good - fine :/khub/ خوب	to speak :/harf zadan/ حَرف زَدَن
self :/khod/ خود	protection :/hefz/ حفظ
to eat :/khordan/ خوردَن	towel :/hôle/ حوله
happy :/khosh'hâl/ خوشحال	yard :/hayât/ حَیاط
delicious :/khoshmaze/ خوشمَزه	thorn :/Khâr/ خار
very :/kheili/ خِیلی	cream :/khâme/ خامه
shout : /dâd/ داد	lady :/khânom/ خانُم
to give :/dâdan/ دادَن	house :/khâne/ خانه
sickle :/dâs/ داس	family :/khânevâde/ خانواده
to own :/dâshtan/ داشتَن	goodbye :/khodâhâfez/ خُداحافظ
wisdom :/dânâyi/ دانایی	maid :/khedmatkâr/ خدمَتکار
science :/dânesh/ دانش	rooster :/khorus/ خُروس
student :/dâneshju/ دانشجو	to buy :/kharidan/ خَریدَن
daughter – girl :/dokhtar/ دُختَر	tired :/khaste/ خَسته
in - door :/darb/ دَر	danger :/khatar/ خَطَر

راست /râst/: straight	دِرَخت /derakht/: tree
راضی /râzi/: satisfied	دَرخواست /darkhâst/: appeal
راندَن /rândan/: to drive	دَرس /dars/: lesson- study
رِساندَن /resândan/: to deliver	دَریا /daryâ/: sea
رِسیدَن /residan/: achieve	دَست /dast/: hand
رَفتَن /raftan/: go	دُم /dom/: tail
رَواج /ravâj/: currency	دوچَرخِه /docharkhe/: bike
رود /rud/: river	دوچَرخِه سَواری /docharkhesavâri/: riding bike
روستا /rustâ/: village	دور /dur/: far
روشَن /rôshan/: bright	دوست /dust/: friend
روشَنایی /rôshanâyi/: light	دوست داشتَن /dust dâshtan/: to like
روی /ruye/: on	دوستان /dustân/: friends
زَبان /zabân/: language	دیدَن /didan/: to see
زَدَن /zadan/: to hit	دیروز /diruz/: yesterday
زَر /zar/: gold	دیگَران /digarân/: others
زِندِگی /zendegi/: life	ذات /zât/: nature
زود /zud/: soon	ذِهن /zehn/: mind
زیاد /ziyâd/: very	

شَب /shab/: night	زیر /zir/: under
شُدَن /shodan/: to become	ژست /zhest/: gusture
شُستَن /shostan/: to wash	ژولیده /zhulideh/: slovenly
شش /shesh/: six	ساختَن /sâkhtan/: to build
شنا /shenâ/: swimming	ساعَت /sâ'at/ : clock - hour
شناختَن /shenâkhtan/: to identify	ساعد /sâed/: forearm
شنیدَن /shenidan/: to listen	ساقه /sâghe/: pedicel
شَهر /shahr/: town	سال /sâl/: year
شیر /shir/: lion - milk	سَبَد /sabad/: basket
صابون /sâbun/: soap	سَبزی /sabzi/: vegetable
صُبح /sobh/: morning	ستاره /setâre/: star
صُبحانه /sobhâne/: breakfast	سَر /sar/: head
صَبر /sabr/: patience	سَردَرد /sardard/: headache
صَد /sad/: hundred	سَعی /sa'y/: effort
صَندَلی /sandali/: chair	سَگ /sag/: dog
صَندوقدار /sandoghdâr/: cashier	سَم /sam/: poison
صورَت /surat/: face	سیاه /siyâh/: black
ضارب /zâreb'/: assailant	شاد /shâd/: happy

181 www.LearnPersianOnline.com

فُروختَن /forukhtan/: to sell	ضربه /zarbe/: hit
فُروشگاه /forushgâh/: store	ضَرَر /zarar/: lost
فُروشنده /forushande/: salesman	طَرح /tarh/: plan
فَقَط /faghat/: only	طَناب /tanâb/: rope
فَهمیدَن /fahmidan/: to realize	طوفان /tufân/: flood
قاشُق /ghâshogh/: spoon	ظالم /zâlem/: cruel
قَشَنگ /ghashang/: beautiful	ظاهر /zâher/: appearance
قَلب /ghalb/: heart	ظَرف /zarf/: dish
قَند /ghand/: sugar	ظُهر /zohr/: noon
قندان /ghandân/: sugar bowl	عَرَب /arab/: Arab
قَهوه /ghahve/: coffee	علم /elm/: science
قیافه /ghiyâfe/: gesture	عَمو /amu/: uncle
قیمَت /gheimat/: price	عید /eid/: festival
کار /kār/: work	غَذا /ghaza/: food
کارمَند /kārmand/: employee	فَراوان /farâvân/: plenty
کَباب /kabāb/: kebab	فَردا /fardâ/: tomorrow
کتاب /ketāb/: book	فرستادَن /ferestâdan/: to send
کَر /kar/: deaf	فَرش /farsh/: carpet

182 www.LearnPersianOnline.com

stork :/laklak/ لَک لَک	to draw :/keshidegi/ کِشیدَن
mother :/mâdar/ مادَر	class :/kelâs/ کلاس
snake :/mâr/ مار	little :/kam/ کَم
to stay :/mândan/ ماندَن	help :/komak/ کُمَک
moon - month :/mâh/ ماه	small :/kuchak/ کوچَک
text :/matn/ مَتن	blind :/kur/ کور
variety :/motenave'/ مُتِنَوِع	cow :/gâv/ گاو
example :/mesâl/ مثال	to put :/gozâshtan/ گُذاشتَن
positive :/mosbat/ مُثبَت	hungry :/gorosne/ گُرُسنه
triangle :/mosalas/ مُثَلَث	to take :/gereftan/ گِرِفتَن
diverse :/mokhtalef/ مُختَلَف	wolf :/gorg/ گُرگ
specific :/makhsus/ مَخصوص	to say :/goftan/ گُفتَن
pencil :/medâd/ مداد	mud :/gel/ گِل
a while :/modati/ مُدَتی	flower :/gol/ گُل
school :/madrese/ مَدرسه	pot :/goldân/ گُلدان
ceremony :/marâsem/ مَراسِم	brawn :/gusht/ گوشت
man :/mard/ مَرد	lip :/lab/ لَب
people :/mardom/ مَردُم	dress :/lebâs/ لِباس

bread :/nân/ نان	to die :/mordan/ مُردَن
lunch :/nâhâr/ ناهار	death :/marg/ مَرگ
rescue :/nejât/ نجات	sick :/mariz/ مَریض
to sit :/neshastan/ نِشَستَن	busy :/mashghul/ مَشغول
painting :/naghâshi/ نَقاشی	confident :/motma'en/ مُطمَئِن
look :/negâh/ نگاه	famous :/ma'ruf/ مَعروف
symbol :/nemâd/ نماد	teacher :/moalem/ مُعَلِم
to write :/neveshtan/ نوِشتَن	place :/makân/ مَکان
same :/hamân/ هَمان	queen :/malake/ مَلَکه
neighbor :/hamsâye/ هَمسایه	I :/man/ مَن
all :/hame/ هَمه	kind :/mehrabân/ مِهرَبان
always :/hamishe/ هَمیشه	mouse :/mush/ موش
art :/honar/ هُنَر	prosperous :/movafagh/ مُوَفَق
artist :/honarmand/ هُنَرمَند	time :/moghe'/ موقِع
amid :/vasat/ وَسَط	table :/miz/ میز
	suddenly :/nâgahân/ ناگَهان
	name :/nâm/ نام
	letter :/nâme/ نامه

ضَمیمِه

Appendix

Most Common Persian Verbs

The following table presents 100 most common Persian verbs and their present and past steams:

Most Common Persian Verbs

Present Steam	Past Steam	English	Pronunciation	Persian
ده (آزار)	آزار داد	tease	âzâr dâdan	آزار دادَن
آی	آمد	come	âmadan	آمَدَن
آموز	آموخت	learn	âmukhtan	آموختَن
آور	آورد	bring	âvardan	آوردَن
ده (اجاره)	اجاره داد	lease	ejâre dâdan	اِجاره دادَن
ده (ارائه)	ارائه داد	exhibit	erâ'e dâdan	اِرائه دادَن
افروز	افروخت	fire	afrukhtan	آفروختَن
افزای	افزود	increase	afzudan	آفزودَن
انداز	انداخت	drop, throw	andâkhtan	آنداختَن
ایست	ایستاد	stop, stand	istâdan	ایستادَن

Most Common Persian Verbs

Present Steam	Past Steam	English	Pronunciation	Persian
بخش	بخشید	grant, forgive	bakhshidan	بَخشیدَن
بردار	برداشت	take, pickup	bardâshtan	بَرداشتَن
بر	برد	win, carry	bordan	بُردَن
برگرد	برگشت	return	bargashtan	بَرگَشتَن
بر	برید	cut, chop	boridan	بُریدَن
بند	بست	shut, tighten	bastan	بَستَن
(بهوش) آی	بهوش آمد	revive	behush âmadan	بِهوش آمَدَن
باش	بود	exist, stand	budan	بودَن
بوس	بوسید	kiss	busidan	بوسیدَن
بوی	بویید	smell	buyidan	بوییدَن
پاش	پاشید	spray, pour	pâshidan	پاشیدَن
پز	پخت	cook	pokhtan	پُختَن

Most Common Persian Verbs

Present Steam	Past Steam	English	Pronunciation	Persian
پذیر	پذیرفت	admit, accept	paziroftan	پَذیرُفتَن
پرداز	پرداخت	pay	pardâkhtan	پَرداختَن
پرس	پرسیدن	ask	porsidan	پُرسیدَن
پسند	پسندید	choose, accept	pasandidan	پَسندیدَن
پوس	پوسید	decay	pusidan	پوسیدَن
پوش	پوشید	wear	pushidan	پوشیدَن
پیچ	پیچید	twist, roll	pichidan	پیچیدَن
پیمای	پیمود	run, pace	peimudan	پِیمودَن
پیوند	پیوست	join, connect	peivastan	پِیوَستَن
ترسان	ترساند	threat, horrify	tarsândan	تَرساندَن
ترس	ترسید	abhor, scare	tarsidan	تَرسیدَن
جه	جست	jump, leap	jostan	جُستَن

Present Steam	Past Steam	English	Pronunciation	Persian
جنب	جنبید	vibrate, move	jonbidan	جُنبیدَن
جوشان	جوشاند	boil	jushândan	جوشاندَن
جوش	جوشید	boil	jushidan	جوشیدَن
جو	جوید	chew	javidan	جَویدَن
چرخ	چرخید	rotate	charkhidan	چَرخیدَن
چسبان	چسباند	stick, paste	chasbândan	چَسباندَن
چسب	چسبید	cohere, cling	chasbidan	چَسبیدَن
چش	چشید	taste	cheshidan	چِشیدَن
چین	چید	pickup	chidan	چیدَن
حل کن	حل کرد	solve	hal kardan	حَل کَردَن
خر	خرید	buy - purchase	kharidan	خَریدَن
خم شو	خم شد	bow, recline	kham shodan	خَم شُدَن

Most Common Persian Verbs

Present Steam	Past Steam	English	Pronunciation	Persian
بین (خواب)	خواب دید	dream	khâb didan	خواب دیدَن
خواب	خوابید	sleep, lie	khâbidan	خوابیدَن
خواه	خواست	ask, desire	khâstan	خواستَن
ده	داد	grant, give	dâdan	دادَن
دار	داشت	own, have	dâshtan	داشتَن
دان	دانست	cognize, know	dânestan	دانِستَن
دوز	دوخت	sew	dukhtan	دوختَن
دو	دوید	run	davidan	دَویدَن
بین	دید	see, observe	didan	دیدَن
ران	راند	drive	rândan	راندَن
رس	رسید	arrive	residan	رِسیدَن
رقص	رقصید	dance	raghsidan	رَقصیدَن

Most Common Persian Verbs

Present Steam	Past Steam	English	Pronunciation	Persian
رنج	رنجید	huff, miff	ranjidan	رَنجیدَن
ریز	ریخت	shed, pour	rikhtan	ریختَن
زای	زایید	birth, bear	zâyidan	زاییدَن
زن	زد	beat, shoot	zadan	زَدَن
ساز	ساخت	establish, build	sâkhtan	ساختَن
سپر	سپرد	depute, entrust	sepordan	سِپُردَن
سنج	سنجید	evaluate	sanjidan	سَنجیدَن
سوز	سوخت	burn	sukhtan	سوختَن
شو	شد	become	shodan	شُدَن
شوی	شست	wash	shostan	شَستَن
شکن	شکستن	break	shekastan	شِکَستَن
شمر	شمرد	count	shemordan	شِمُردَن

Most Common Persian Verbs

Present Steam	Past Steam	English	Pronunciation	Persian
شناس	شناخت	identify	shenâkhtan	شِناخَتَن
شنو	شنید	hear	shenidan	شِنیدَن
غلت	غلتید	roll	ghaltidan	غَلتیدَن
فرست	فرستاد	forward, send	ferestâdan	فِرستادَن
فرمای	فرمود	bid	farmudan	فَرمودَن
فرو بر	فرو برد	plunge	foru bordan	فُرو بُردَن
فروش	فروخت	sell	forukhtan	فُروختَن
فشر	فشرد	squeeze	feshordan	فِشُردَن
فهم	فهمید	understand	fahmidan	فَهمیدَن
کار	کاشت	implant	kâshtan	کاشتَن
کن	کرد	do, perform	kardan	کَردَن
کش	کشت	kill, murder	koshtan	کُشتَن

8 www.LearnPersianOnline.com

Most Common Persian Verbs

Present Steam	Past Steam	English	Pronunciation	Persian
کش	کشید	pull, drag	keshidan	کِشیدَن
کن	کند	dig, peel	kandan	کَندَن
کوب	کوبید	hammer, bruise	kubidan	کوبیدَن
گذار	گذاشتن	put, let	gozâshtan	گُذاشتَن
گیر	گرفت	take, hold	gereftan	گِرِفتَن
گریز	گریخت	escape	gorikhtan	گُریختَن
گرد	گشت	roll, search	gashtan	گَشتَن
گو	گفت	say, tell	goftan	گُفتَن
لرز	لرزید	vibrate, shake	larzidan	لَرزیدَن
مان	ماند	stay, stand	mândan	ماندَن
میر	مرد	dying	mordan	مُردَن
نال	نالید	complain	nâlidan	نالیدَن

Most Common Persian Verbs

Present Steam	Past Steam	English	Pronunciation	Persian
نشین	نشست	sit	neshastan	نِشَستَن
(نگاه) کن	نگاه کرد	see, look	negâh kardan	نِگاه کَردَن
نگهدار	نگهداشت	hold	negahdâshtan	نگَهداشتَن
نویس	نوشت	write	neveshtan	نِوِشتَن
وز	وزید	blow	vazidan	وَزیدَن
یاب	یافت	find, discover	yâftan	یافتَن

Persian Most Common Words

Family		خانواده /khânevâde/
English	**Pronunciation**	**Persian**
Mother	mâdar	مادر
Father	pedar	پدر
Brother	barâdar	برادر
Sister	khâhar	خواهر
Grandfather	pedar bozorg	پدربزرگ
Grandmother	mâdar bozorg	مادربزرگ
Grandchild	nave	نوه
Son	pesar	پسر
Daughter	dokhtar	دختر
Children	bachehâ	بچه ها

Family خانواده

/khânevâde/

English	Pronunciation	Persian
Wife, Woman	zan	زن
Husband	shohar	شوهر
Uncle (Father's brother)	amu	عمو
Uncle (Mother's brother)	dâyi	دایی
Aunt (Mother' sister)	khâle	خاله
Aunt (Father's sister)	ame	عمه
Brother-in-law (Wife's brother)	barâdar zan	برادر زن
Sister-in-law (Wife's sister)	khahar zan	خواهر زن
Sister-in-law (husband's sister)	khâhar shohar	خواهر شوهر
Sister-in-law (brother's wife)	zane barâdar	زن برادر

Family /khânevâde/ خانواده

English	Pronunciation	Persian
Mother-in-law (Wife's mother)	mâdarzan	مادرزن
Mother-in-law (Husband's mother)	mâdarshohar	مادرشوهر
Nephew/niece (sister's child)	khâharzâde	خواهرزاده
Nephew/niece (brother's child)	barâdarzâde	برادرزاده
Son-in-law	dâmâd	داماد

Weather / آب و هوا
/âbo havâ/

English	Pronunciation	Persian
Atmosphere	jav	جو
Cloudy	abri	ابری
Cold	sard	سرد
Cyclone, Vortex	gerdbâd	گردباد
Dust storm	tufâne gardo khâk	طوفان گردوخاک
Evaporation	tabkhir	تبخیر
Fog	meh	مه
Hail	tagarg	تگرگ
Heat	garmâ	گرما
Ice	yakh	یخ
Nice day	ruze khub	روز خوب
Rain	barun	باران
Rainbow	rangin kamân	رنگین کمان

Weather / آب و هوا

/âbo havâ/

English	Pronunciation	Persian
Raining	barun miyâd	باران میاد
Severe weather	havâye bad	هوای بد
Sky	âsemân	آسمان
Snow	barf	برف
Snowing.	barf miyâd	برف میاد
Storm	tufân	توفان
Sun	khorshid	خورشید
Sunny	âftâbi	آفتابی
Thunderstorm	tufân - ra'do bargh	رعد و برق
Warm	garm	گرم
Wind	bâd	باد

Colors

رنگ ها

/ranghâ/

English	Pronunciation	Persian
Aqua	firuze'i	فیروزه‌ای
Aquamarine	yashmi	یشمی
Bisque	kerem	کرم
Black	siyâh	سیاه
Blue	âbi	آبی
Brown	ghahve'i	قهوه‌ای
Coral	bezh	بژ
Crimson	zereshki	زرشکی
Dark Blue	sorme'i	سرمه‌ای
Dodger Blue	nili	نیلی
Gray	khâkestari	خاکستری
Green	sabz	سبز

Colors

رنگ ها

/ranghâ/

English	Pronunciation	Persian
Maroon	âlbâluyi	آلبالویی
Navy	lâjevardi	لاجوردی
Orange	nârenji	نارنجی
Pink	surati	صورتی
Purple	arghavâni	ارغوانی
Red	ghermez	قرمز
Violet	banafsh	بنفش
White	sefid	سفید
Yellow	zard	زرد

Animals /heyvânât/ حیوانات

English	Pronunciation	Persian
Alligator	temsâh	تمساح
Anteater	murchekhâr	مورچه خوار
Bat	khofâsh	خفاش
Bear	khers	خرس
Beaver	sage âbi	سگ آبی
Bull	gave nar	گاو نر
Calf	gusâle	گوساله
Camel	shotor	شتر
Cat	gorbe	گربه
Cow	gâve made	گاو ماده
Crocodile	susmâr	سوسمار
Dog	sag	سگ
Donkey	khar	خر

Animals

حیوانات

/heyvânât/

English	Pronunciation	Persian
Elephant	fil	فیل
Fox	rubâh	روباه
Giraffe	zarâfe	زرافه
Goat	boz	بز
Horse	asb	اسب
Leopard	palang	پلنگ
Lion	shir	شیر
Monkey	meymun	میمون
Mouse	mush	موش
Pig	khuk	خوک
Rabbit	khargush	خرگوش
Sheep	gusfand	گوسفند
Snake	mâr	مار

		حیوانات
	Animals	
		/heyvânât/
English	**Pronunciation**	**Persian**
Squirrel	sanjâb	سنجاب
Tiger	babr	ببر
Tortoise	lâkposht	لاک پشت
Wolf	gorg	گرگ

Fruits/Vegetables

میوه ها/سبزیجات

/mivehâ – sabzijât/

English	Pronunciation	Persian
Apples	sib	سیب
Apricots	zardâlu	زردآلو
Bananas	môz	موز
Beans	lubiyâ	لوبیا
Blueberries	zoghâl akhte	زغال اخته
Cabbage	kalam	کلم
Carrots	havij	هویج
Cauliflower	gole kalam	گل کلم
Celery	karafs	کرفس
Cherries	gilâs	گیلاس
Corn	zorat	ذرت
Cucumbers	khiyâr	خیار
Eggplant	bâdemjun	بادمجان

Fruits/Vegetables — میوه ها/سبزیجات

/mivehâ – sabzijât/

English	Pronunciation	Persian
Figs	anjir	انجیر
Grapes	angur	انگور
Green beans	lubiyâ sabz	لوبیا سبز
Kiwi	kivi	کیوی
Lemons	limu	لیمو
Lettuce	kâhu	کاهو
Lime	limu torgh	لیمو ترش
Mangos	anbe	انبه
Mushrooms	ghârch	قارچ
Olives	zeytun	زیتون
Onions	piyâz	پیاز
Oranges	porteghal	پرتقال
Peaches	holu	هلو

English	Pronunciation	Persian
Fruits/Vegetables		**میوه ها/سبزیجات** /mivehâ – sabzijât/
Pears	golâbi	گلابی
Peas	nokhod farangi	نخود فرنگی
Pickles	khiyâr shur	خیار شور
Potato	sibzamini	سیب زمینی
Raisins	keshmesh	کشمش
Strawberries	tut farangi	توت فرنگی
Tangerines	nârangi	نارنگی
Tomatoes	goje farangi	گوجه فرنگی
Vegetables	sabzijât	سبزیجات
Watermelons	hendevâne	هندوانه
Zucchini	kadu	کدو

Jobs / شغل ها /shoghlhâ/

English	Pronunciation	Persian
Actress, actor	honarpishe	هنر پیشه
Artist	honarmand	هنرمند
Baker	nânvâ	نانوا
Banker	bânkdâr	بانکدار
Barber	ârâyeshgar	آرایشگر
Blacksmith	âhangar	آهنگر
Carpenter	najâr	نجار
Cashier	sandughdâr	صندوقدار
Chef	sarâshpaz	سرآشپز
Clerk	kârmand	کارمند
Coach	morabi	مربی (ورزشی)
Cook	âshpaz	آشپز
Dentist	dandânpezeshk	دندان پزشک
Detective	kârâgâh	کارگاه
Doctor	doctor	دکتر
Dress maker, tailor	khayâte	خیاط
Driver	rânande	راننده
Employee	kârmand	کارمند
Engineer	mohandes	مهندس

Jobs		شغل ها /shoghlhâ/
English	**Pronunciation**	**Persian**
Farmer	keshâvarz	کشاورز
Guard	negahbân	نگهبان
Housekeeper	khânedâr	خانه دار
Housekeeper	khânedâr	خانه دار
Hunter	shekârchi	شکارچی

Other books of Interest

Learn Farsi in 100 Days

The Ultimate Crash Course to Learning Farsi Fast

The goal of this book is simple. It will help you incorporate the best method and the right strategies to learn Farsi FAST and EFFECTIVELY.

Learn Farsi in 100 days helps you learn speak Farsi faster than you ever thought possible. You only need to spend about 90-120 minutes daily in your 100-day period in order to learn Farsi language at advanced level. Whether you are just starting to get in touch the Farsi language, or even if you have already learned the basics of the language, this book can help you accelerate the learning process and put you on the right track.

Learn Farsi in 100 days is for Farsi learners from the beginning to the advanced level. It is a breakthrough in Farsi language learning — offering a winning formula and the most powerful methods for learning to speak Farsi fluently and confidently. Each contains 4 pages covering a comprehensive range of topics. Each day includes vocabulary, grammar, reading and writing lessons. It gives learners easy access to the Farsi vocabulary and grammar as it is actually used in a comprehensive range of everyday life situations and it teaches students to use Farsi for situations related to work, social life, and leisure. Topics such as greetings, family, weather, sports, food, customs, etc. are presented in interesting unique ways using real-life information.

Purchase on Amazon website:

https://goo.gl/eG2n11

Published By:
LearnPersianOnline.com

Farsi Conversations
Learn the Most Common Words and Phrases Farsi Speakers use Every Day

Learning about a new culture is always an exciting prospect and one of the best ways to get to know about another country, its people and their customs, is to learn the language.

Now, with Farsi Conversations: Learn the Most Common Words and Phrases Farsi Speakers use Every Day you can learn how to communicate in Farsi and learn more about Persian culture at the same time.

In this unique guide, you will be able to practice your spoken Farsi with FREE YouTube videos. It is an ideal tool for learners of Farsi at all levels, whether at school, in evening classes or at home, and is a 'must have' for business or leisure.

Farsi students can learn;

- How to use the right language structures and idioms in the right context
- Practice Farsi vocabulary and phrases needed in everyday situations
- Gain proficiency in written and spoken Farsi
- New ways of mastering Farsi phrases

By the end of the book you will have learned more than 2500 Farsi words, have mastered more than 300 commonly used Farsi verbs, key expressions and phrases and be able to pose more than 800 questions.

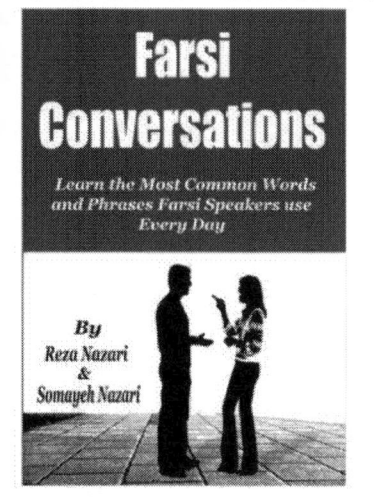

Purchase on Amazon website:

https://goo.gl/bGpVNZ

Published By:
LearnPersianOnline.com

The Only Book You Ever Need To Master Persian Language

Learn to Speak Persian Fast is a multi-level series for Persian learners from the beginning to the advanced level. It is a breakthrough in Persian language learning — offering a winning formula and the most powerful methods for learning to speak Persian fluently and confidently. Each book provides 10 chapters covering a comprehensive range of topics. Each chapter includes vocabulary, grammar, reading and writing lessons.

Book 1 of Learn to Speak Persian Fast series is designed for beginning students needing a comprehensive, slow-paced arrangement of basic pronunciation, grammar structures, and vocabulary. It gives learners easy access to the Persian vocabulary and grammar as it is actually used in a comprehensive range of everyday life situations and it teaches students to use Persian for situations related to work, social life, and leisure.

LearnPersianOnline.com

The only Farsi Grammar Book You'll Ever Need!

Farsi Grammar in Use is a series of three volumes.

This volume is for students at beginners level.

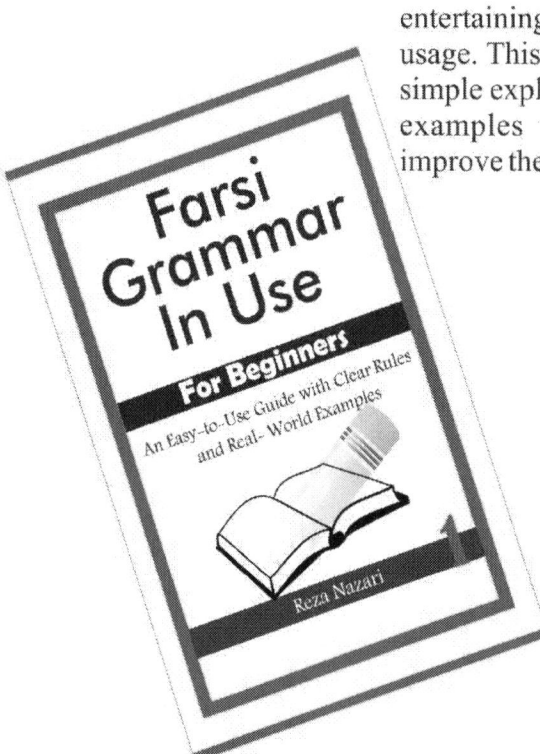

Farsi Grammar in Use is a concise and entertaining guide to Farsi grammar and usage. This user-friendly resource includes simple explanations of grammar and useful examples to help students of all ages improve their Farsi.

Appropriate for any age range, this easy-to-follow guide makes learning Farsi grammar and usage simple and fun.

For anyone who wants to understand the major rules and subtle guidelines of Farsi grammar and usage, *Farsi Grammar in Use* offers comprehensive straightforward instruction.

It covers a wide range of subjects as they are taught in many language schools around the world.

LearnPersianOnline.com

Most Common
Persian Verbs

200 Essential Persian Verbs is the only reference you need to master Persian most common verbs. This book will help you learn verb conjugating, usage, phrasal verbs, and even the roots of verbs, both present and past.

This book is not just another reference list of verbs. It shows the depth of variation and irregularity among Persian verbs, and it groups similar verbs together to make the patterns behind them easier to learn. Verbs in this book are arranged from least popular to most.

Inside you'll find:

Hundreds of example sentences showing verbs in action

An easy-to-use format for both quick reference and in-depth study

Synonyms and Antonyms listed for each of the model Persian verbs

200 most common Persian verbs, their meanings and pronunciation guide

Essential Phrases You'll Need to Know Before Your Trip

Persian for busy travelers is a book for tourists and business people.

It is for those who travel to Iran, Afghanistan and Tajikistan. Designed as a quick reference and study guide, this book is structured for quick access to phrases related to basic phrases, transportation, shopping, and other common circumstances. A phonetic pronunciation accompanies each phrase.

This concise phrasebook gives business and vacation travelers everything they need for a smooth, successful trip. Organized by subject, you can quickly find the vocabulary relevant to the situation accompanied by a pronunciation guide.

LearnPersianOnline.com

Lists of the Most Relevant
Persian Vocabulary

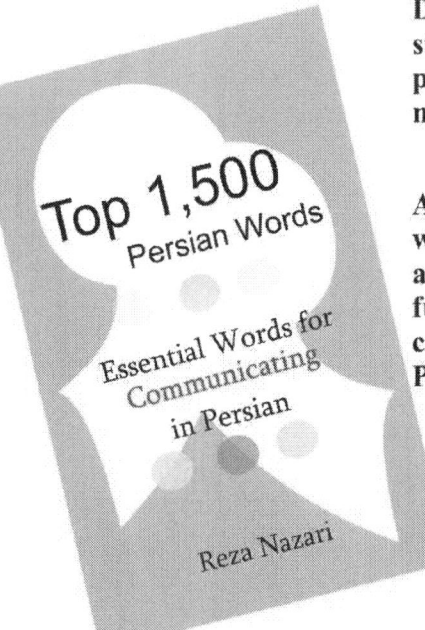

Designed as a quick reference and study guide, this reference book provides easy-to-learn lists of the most relevant Persian vocabulary.

Arranged by 36 categories, these word lists furnish the reader with an invaluable knowledge of fundamental vocabulary to comprehend, read, write and speak Persian.

Top 1,500 Persian Words
Essential Words for Communicating in Persian
Reza Nazari

Top 1,500 Persian Words is intended to teach the essentials of Persian quickly and effectively.

The common words are organized to enable the reader to handle day to day situations. Words are arranged by topic, such as family, jobs, weather, numbers, countries, sports, common verbs, etc. A phonetic pronunciation accompanies each word.

A Guidance for Communication in Persian

Designed as a quick reference and study guide, this comprehensive phrasebook offers guidance for situations including traveling, accommodations, healthcare, emergencies and other common circumstances.

Easy Persian Phrasebook is designed to teach the essentials of Persian quickly and effectively.

The book should suit anyone who needs to get to grips quickly with Persian, such as tourists and business travelers.

Essential Expressions for Communicating in Persian

A comprehensive Farsi - English dictionary

Designed for people interested in learning standard Farsi, this comprehensive dictionary of the Farsi-English languages contains more than 12,000 entries and definitions as well as pronunciation guides, word types, Current phrases, slang, idioms, scientific terms and other features.

The Dictionary is fully updated with the latest lexical content. It's a unique database that offers the fullest, most accurate picture of the Farsi language today. Hundreds of new words cover technology, computing, ecology, and many other subjects.

Fully updated with the latest lexical content.

Offers more than 12,000 Farsi entries.

A unique database that offers the fullest, most accurate picture of the Farsi language today.

Contains pronunciation guides, word types, slangs, idioms, scientific terms and other features.

Hundreds of new words cover technology, computing, ecology, and many other subjects.

Most Popular Farsi Idioms

Idioms with Their English Equivalents

This handy book is a collection of 300 most popular Farsi idioms used in everyday context with their best equivalents in English. The idioms provided here can help the keen learner broaden their knowledge of the Farsi language and culture.

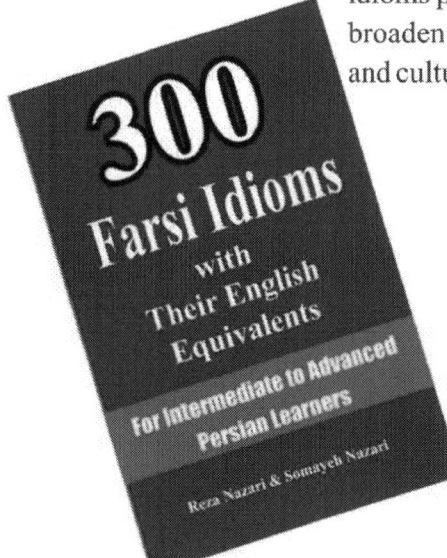

Farsi speaking natives love to use idioms. The Essential idioms in this book offer an additional look at the idiomatic phrases and sayings that make Farsi the rich language that it is.

A compilation of 300 most popular Farsi idioms widely used in Iran in everyday context with their best English equivalents are presented with illustrations so that learners using this section will have many idioms 'at their fingertips'.

LearnPersianOnline.com

"learn Persian Online" Publications

Learn Persian Online authors' team strives to prepare and publish the best quality Persian Language learning resources to make learning Persian easier for all. We hope that our publications help you learn this lovely language in an effective way.

Please let us know how your studies turn out. We would like to know what part of our books worked for you and how we can make these books better for others. You can reach us via email at info@learnpersianonline.com

We all in Learn Persian Online wish you good luck and successful studies!

Learn Persian Online Authors

Best Persian Learning Books

Published By:
LearnPersianOnline.com

Learn to Speak Persian Online

Enjoy interactive Persian lessons on Skype with the best native speaking Persian teachers

Online Persian Learning that's Effective, Affordable, Flexible, and Fun.

Learn Persian wherever you want; when you want

Ultimate flexibility. You can now learn Persian online via Skype, enjoy high quality engaging lessons no matter where in the world you are. It's affordable too.

Learn Persian With One-on-One Classes

We provide one-on-one Persian language tutoring online, via Skype. We believe that one-to-one tutoring is the most effective way to learn Persian.

Qualified Native Persian Tutors

Working with the best Persian tutors in the world is the key to success! Our Persian tutors give you the support & motivation you need to succeed with a personal touch.

It's easy! Here's how it works

Request a FREE introductory session
Meet a Persian tutor online via Skype
Start speaking Real Persian in Minutes

Send Email to: info@LearnPersianOnline.com

Or Call: +1-469-230-3605